PUBS OF DEVON

Edited by R M Smith

Introduction by Jeremy Bates
Illustrated by Myerscough

BAYARD LONDON

First published in Britain in 1975
Sponsored by Miles Laboratories Limited
makers of Alka-Seltzer

ISBN 0 220 66655 5

This book has been set 10pt Univers Medium, prepared for press by
The Ivory Head Press, 170 Murray Road, London W5, and printed
in England by Redwood Burn Limited, Trowbridge and Esher,
for the publishers, Bayard Books
Registered office: 110 Fleet Street, London EC4A 2JL
Publishing office: c/o Business Books Limited, Mercury House,
Waterloo Road, London SE1 8UL

Front cover: Fishermans Cott, Bickleigh

This book is sponsored by
MILES LABORATORIES LIMITED of
Stoke Court, Stoke Poges, Slough, Buckinghamshire
makers of
ALKA-SELTZER

Stoke Court, Stoke Poges

Stoke Court, the UK headquarters of Miles Laboratories, was originally
built in 1641. Leased to an uncle and aunt of Thomas Gray, the poet,
1742 saw the arrival at the house of Thomas' mother, Dorothy. During
Thomas' vacations from Cambridge he stayed at Stoke Court where
he put the finishing touches to his poems "Ode on a distant prospect of
Eton College" and "Elegy, written in a Country Churchyard".

After his mother's death, Thomas gave up the lease to Stoke Court and the
house passed through various hands and fortunes for the following
century. But in 1844 it was bought by Granville Penn, grandson of William
Penn, founder of Pennsylvania. Under the directorship of Granville's
son Stoke Court was enlarged and improved and the frontage given a mock
Tudor appearance. Throughout the improvements, however, great care was
taken not to change the style of the rooms that had been used by Gray.

From the middle of the **19**th century Stoke Court again passed through
varying fortunes being used in turn as private house, country club and
warehouse. It was allowed to fall into a derelict state and was ready for
demolition when Miles Laboratories bought the house in 1958. The
company has painstakingly restored Stoke Court to its previous magnificence
and in doing so has preserved a part of the heritage of England.

Preface

Pubs included in this volume have been chosen for their atmosphere, historic interest, setting and general standard of food, drink and amenities. No payment for inclusion is involved.

Pubs of Devon is conveniently arranged and indexed for easy use. Compiled alphabetically under the town or village in which they are situated, each pub has a reference number. The reference numbers are repeated on the map of Devon, found on pages 48 and 49, to enable visitors to the county to locate pubs easily. These numbers are repeated in the alphabetical index at the back of the book. Information on location, food and drinks available, accommodation, exterior appearance, interior atmosphere, setting, items of historic interest, local attractions are given for each pub.

The information has been compiled either from the landlords of the establishments concerned or from personal visits. Every effort has been made to ensure accuracy, but the publishers cannot accept responsibility for any errors that may have occurred.

The Editor, would, however, be pleased to hear from anyone who has suggestions for pubs to be included in later editions and from anyone who has constructive criticisms to make.

R.M.S.

Contents

Introduction

Devon is the most beautiful and varied county in England, for nowhere is more typical of our Motherland than this county of little towns and quaint sea-ports. It is a paradise of simple beauties, green fields, quiet lanes, fast flowing rivers and hundreds of small villages, each with its own picturesque pub.

She is a mighty county in spirit and size, and is spread over 2610 square miles. Devon has two distinct coastlines, the northern shore having a rugged grandeur against which the Atlantic thrusts its never-ending rollers, whilst the south, with its green hills and red cliffs facing the more gentle English Channel, has an individual scenic beauty.

Between the two lie the great tracts of Exmoor and Dartmoor, both having their own distinctive features and historic origins. All this, laced with varied river estuaries, some of which on a full tide seem like great lakes, make the county truly glorious.

Both the geography and topography of Devon are rather complicated. The heart of the county is the granite mass of Dartmoor, rising in two places, High Willhays and Yes Tor, to just over 2000 feet above sea level. Exmoor, if less imposing is a most gentle moorland, which some find more attractive. Outside the two moors, many hills rise to 8 or 900 feet and command magnificent views, the finest perhaps from Haldon, the range of hills to the west of Exeter.

Devon has a rich history, evidence of which can be seen in the relics of the Stone Age and pre-historic man at Kents Cavern, Torquay. These caves were hollowed out of the limestone, thousands of years ago and have been the home of man and many pre-historic beasts, including the mammoth, the sabre-toothed tiger, the cave lion and the woolly rhinoceros. In nearby Brixham similar caves have been found, with the remains of a submerged forest.

Other parts of the county's heritage have been revealed in the remains of the Bronze Age settlements to be found on many parts of Dartmoor. Celts, Romans, Saxons and Normans have all in turn made their home in Exeter beside the once important River Exe. The Romans were the first to make a fortress here and it is believed that William the Conqueror also chose the same site on which to build his castle. He called it Rougemont (the Red Hill) commemorating Devon's rich red soil.

Devon was the home of the great Elizabethan explorers who colonised the New World. Drake, Raleigh, Grenville, Frobisher, Hawkins, Gilbert and Davies are among the most famous. Let us not forget, it was Devon men who first sailed round the world, and who established our oldest colony. Their names and deeds are recorded in history books, but their ancestral homes can be visited across the county, many will even now be licensed, and entertain travellers from the New World as well as the old.

A count in Elizabethan England revealed that with a population of only 4000000 , nearly 20000 ale-house licenses had been issued. The Victorian era boasts just over 118000 licensed premises supplying the nation's needs, making our present day total of 73000 sound very meagre.

Traditionally, pubs have played an important part in the Englishman's way of life, for it is the ideal location for meeting friends and discussing news and views. The British pub has a long and proud tradition and the atmosphere we create inside is the envy of the rest of the world. Since the war the image of our pubs has been revolutionised. Today the food is almost as important as the beer. It was like that, indeed, in earlier centuries, too, but no doubt our grandfathers would turn in their graves if they could see cream cakes and coffee passing over the bar.

Devon's public houses have such charm that no innovator could choose but to retain their original character. Locals battle hard to make sure no city architects or big breweries are allowed to destroy each pub's personality.

So let us now look at some of these delightful pubs and places of interest to the visitor. We start in north Devon near the boundary with Somerset. Ten miles west of Porlock off the A39 is the small village of Lynmouth, a place much loved by Shelley, and the place where Blackmore wrote his novel *Lorna Doone.* It is little more than a string of white painted cottages terraced down the banks of the River Lyn. One of these is the *Rising Sun* that dates back several centuries. There can be few more pleasurable pastimes than to sit on the oak seat outside with a glass of ale, contentedly watching the boats in the snug harbour.

Travelling west on the A339, Combe Martin is the next village of interest, for in the very long main street is one of Devon's strangest houses. When an 18th century squire won a fortune at cards, he resolved to build an appropriate monument, a house. It consisted of four floors, one for each card suit, and on each floor there were thirteen windows. Since his death in 1716 the house has been an inn, aptly called the *Pack of Cards.*

North Devon's most popular resort with holiday visitors is Ilfracombe, situated on an impressive piece of our Atlantic coastline, with its natural harbour, towering cliffs and hills. Overlooking the harbour on Lantern Hill is a strange building — half chapel, half lighthouse. Originally a chapel, in Henry VIII's day it was converted into a lighthouse, when indulgences were granted to penitent people willing to keep the light burning. Nearby is Chambercombe Farm, one of England's oldest manor houses. Steeped in over 800 years of history, it has much to offer the interested visitor.

Continuing in a south-westerly direction we come to Woolacombe, with its long stretches of glorious sand and views as far as Lundy Island. This area is ever popular with surfers during the summer months. Then onto Barnstaple, a bustling town of some importance to the farming communities of the area. It claims to be one of the oldest boroughs in England, with many historic buildings of interest. It stands where the Yeo stream joins the River Taw, which is crossed by means of a 13th century bridge of 16 arches. The town is situated eight miles from the sea and is proud of its traditional market, which has prospered from mediaeval times.

In Elizabethan times, Bideford, too, was a strategic port. From the quay
sailed five ships which joined Drake's fleet to destroy the Spanish Armada,
also an expedition to colonise Raleigh's Virginia. Bideford was a town of
tobacco merchants and seamen, the most famous of whom was Sir Richard
Grenville. It was also the home of Charles Kingsley, author of *Westward Ho!*

One can understand how the taverns must have drawn the adventurous
Elizabethan sailors when they returned from the New World, and how the
simple peasants must have listened with bated breath to the adventurers
talking about their voyages. They would probably have enjoyed an
evening at *Hoops Inn*, just five miles from Bideford on the A39, where
the home-brewed ale was famous. Outside of the *Hoops Inn* today is the
stage coach that plied on this route and deposited its passengers for rest
and refreshments here.

Clovelly, an old fishing village, is one of the loveliest corners of the county.
Its narrow cobbled street goes tumbling down for half a mile to the sea,
lined with beautifully kept cottages. All motor traffic is barred. At the
foot of the street is the harbour, with a stone pier which dates back 500
years.

Just six miles from the Cornish boundary is the famous Hartland Point,
rising steeply 350 feet out of the sea. Its lighthouse can be seen for 20 miles.
South of this point is the county boundary which then runs southwards
along the River Tamar to Plymouth.

Nearly all Devon towns began as settlements chosen because of their proxi-
mity to water. Great Torrington is no exception, for it is right on top of the
River Torridge. During the Civil War the armies crossed Devon several times.
On one occasion General Fairfax took the Royalists by surprise and captured the town of Torrington. His prisoners were locked away for safety in
the old tower of the church, in what had been the Royalist Arsenal. Some-
how the powder was ignited and there was a terrible explosion which
killed 200 men and shattered the church.

It is well worth a walk to the old battlements on Castle Hill, for from
there is a fine view of the Torridge. Beyond the river can be seen the
tower of the 15th century church at Little Torrington, and away to the
right is a place of pathetic memories — Taddiport. This hamlet was once a
leper colony and the little 14th century church of the leper hospital still
stands.

Further south lie two of the largest towns on Dartmoor — the Stannary,
or tin, town of Tavistock and the market town of Okehampton. The
moors rise menacingly behind Okehampton and it is an excellent centre
for persons wishing to lose themselves on Dartmoor, for within a few
miles rise the highest Tors in Devon.

One of the most popular pubs in the area is the *Oxenham Arms* at South
Zeal. Lay monks erected the original building in the 12th century, around
an ancient monolith stone which is still there today. Once a dower house
of the Burgoyne family, the inn has a granite fireplace and granite pillars
support the old oak beams. This inn was well known to the author and

playwright Eden Phillpots who describes it as 'the stateliest and most ancient abode in the hamlet'.

Tavistock has more claim to fame than just being the birthplace of Francis Drake, for it is believed to be one of the longest inhabited parts of the county because of the good supplies of tin to be found on the surface. 100 years before William the Conqueror, Tavistock was a military post on the River Tavy. Later it acquired an Abbey, with a rich centre of religious life.

Henry VIII, we know, broke up all the monastries and sold the estates. To John, Lord Russell, First Earl of Bedford, came Tavistock Abbey. A 19th century Russell rebuilt the town, on advanced town planning principles, to make it the lovely spacious place it is today. Here, too, Francis Drake was born, and his statue can be seen a little way from the main square on the Plymouth road.

Situated 15 miles south of Tavistock is Plymouth, much rebuilt since the war. It incorporates Devonport and its great naval dockyard. Today the city is the largest west of Bristol, and is a bustling commercial centre with a population of over 200000.

The Hoe, famed for the game of bowls Sir Francis Drake insisted on finishing before dealing with the Spanish Armada in 1588, compensates for the lack of sandy beaches at Plymouth. Set on a long, grassy hillside it has sweeping views over Plymouth Sound and as far away as Eddystone Lighthouse. Lying to the east of the Hoe is Sutton Harbour and the Barbican, the oldest part of Plymouth. The narrow old streets lead down to a waterfront full of activity.

Commemorative plaques to the famous voyages that have left this quay can be seen on the Mayflower steps. So many voyages of discovery and colonisation have emanated from the city that there are now 43 other Plymouths around the world. To the west of the city, the River Tamar is spanned by Brunel's railway masterpiece, and by a suspension bridge 1848 feet long.

East of Plymouth is an area of outstanding beauty known as the South Hams, a district of quiet villages, delightful coves and still creeks. Nowhere in Britain does the character of the foreshore alter so rapidly, and as frequently as on this coast of spectacular, wave-pounded cliffs, long beaches and sandy coves.

A typical Devonian hamlet is Kingston, with its own pub called the *Dolphin Inn.* This pub is composed of several terraced cottages joined together and the deeds of the premises date back to 1550 and 1580. When the landlord wanted to expand further, he bought an old hayloft across the road which is now called the *Tallet Bar,* 'tallet' being an old Devon name for hayloft. So the *Dolphin* now has the distinction of being one of the few pubs with a road running through the middle of it.

Nearby is the yachtsman's paradise of Salcombe, a busy port in the 19th century specialising in the building and operation of fast schooners running the fruit trade with Spain in Portugal. It was here that Tennyson was

inspired to write his famous poem *Crossing the Bar.* In the narrow streets
of the village is an abundance of pubs and restaurants, and the foreshore
walks, among the quays and jetties, make it worthwhile leaving the car.
Salcombe lies at the mouth of the estuary. At its furthest inland point is
the ancient market town of Kingsbridge. Back to the coast, and east
again, do not miss that most southerly pub in the county, the *Pig's Nose,*
at the tiny hamlet of East Prawle.

Dartmouth has a unique charm, with its ancient buildings and long quayside fronting the river. This is the home of the Royal Naval College and is
an important mooring place for yachts, as it was for the older ships of the
sailing navy and mercantile marine. To protect the harbour from Breton
raids, a castle was built between 1480 and 1500. This castle is the guardian
of the enchanting River Dart, one of the most delightful waterways in
Devon. Twisting between wooded hills, it takes in the peaceful villages of
Stoke Gabriel and Dittisham on its way upstream to Totnes.

At the navigable limit of the Dart lies the historic town of Totnes. It is little
more than one long street climbing up to a Norman Castle. In a strategic
position at the bottom of the High Street is an old, interesting coaching
inn, the *Royal Seven Stars,* with an unusual room situated over its porch.
Five miles south from Totnes is Torbay. Torbay consists of three towns,
Torquay the Riviera of England, Paignton the family resort, and Brixham
the fishing town.

At one time Brixham was the most important fishing port in the country,
and it still has a large fleet of trawlers. The gaily painted cottages perched
on the hillsides around the harbour provide an attractive setting which is
probably why the quays are always crowded in the summer months with
artists and visitors.

Torquay, with its hotels, restaurants and shops, is one of the busiest
holiday resorts in the west country. Although this area is heavily
populated through the summer season, it is very easy to slip away through
country lanes to quieter villages which have retained their charm and
peaceful atmosphere. In each village there is the inevitable pub which
aims to satisfy the hungry as well as thirsty traveller.

In all Devon's beauty, both natural and man-made, there is one place
that draws the visitor back, that is the Cathedral at Exeter. It was
built in the 12th and 14th centuries and has the largest roof ever built in
the pointed style of architecture. The Cathedral stands in a most beautiful
close of lawns and old buildings of interest.

Visitors come to Devon to see lovely countryside and quaint villages with
traditional pubs. They are never disappointed, for there is an abundance
of all.

Jeremy Bates.

Alka-Seltzer

the speediest possible relief from
Headache with Upset Stomach
from too much to eat or drink

Ashburton

THE EXETER INN

26 West Street, Ashburton, Nr Newton Abbot. Tel: Ashburton 52559

Free House

Map reference number: 47
Situated in the ancient town of Ashburton just off the A38, 10 miles from
Newton Abbot.

Car park. Coaches by appointment. Children's room. Bed & breakfast
available in 2 family and 1 double room.

Keg Toby, Worthington E, Double Diamond and draught Bass, Whitbread
Tankard, M & B mild and Carling lager. Basket meals served over the bar.
A la carte menu available in the separate restaurant.

An attractive 17th century black and white building — though parts are said
to date from 1150 — with bow-fronted windows and an unusual pointed
roof. *The Exeter* has many interesting historical associations. The Baron's
Court and Court Leat were held here during the 18th century, and Sir Walter
Raleigh is believed to have been arrested here in 1603 before being taken to
the Tower of London. Up until 50 years ago horses were brought through the
pub for stabling at the rear.

The interior has been recently renovated. The 2 bars are decorated with
natural stained woodwork, open log fires with copper canopies and exposed
beams.

The town of Ashburton, in which the pub stands, is one of Devon's Stannery
— or tin — towns and was granted a charter in 1285 by Edward 1.

Aveton Gifford

EBB TIDE HOTEL
Aveton Gifford, Nr Kingsbridge. Tel: Loddiswell 284

Free House

Map reference number: 36
Situated on the main A379 to Plymouth in the Avon Valley, 2 miles from
Kingsbridge.

Car park. Coaches welcome. Bed & breakfast available in rooms for 16
adults, all with hot & cold water.

Wide selection of draught and bottled beers available. Snacks served over the
bar and full meals available in the separate restaurant.

The *Ebb Tide* has been for 200 years a well-known and loved landmark on
the bank of the River Avon. There are 3 bars, all with log fires and comfortably furnished.

Glorious scenery, salmon fishing, boating, riding, golf, tennis and swimming
are a selection of the numerous local attractions.

Avonwick

THE AVON INN
Avonwick, South Brent. Tel: South Brent 3475

Bass Charrington

Map reference number: 30
Stiuated on the B3210 Plymouth to Totnes road, 6 miles from Totnes
and 16 miles from Plymouth.

Car park. Coaches by appointment. Large lawn garden with tables and
chairs. Suitable for children. Bed & breakfast available in 3 rooms.
Paddock behind car park for touring caravans.

Draught Bass, keg Worthington E, mild, lager and apple wine available.
Recommended by CAMRA in 1974. Pasties, pies, salads, sandwiches and
various hot meals served over the bar.

On lease to Bass, it is the present owner, Charles Swallow, who presides
over *The Avon.* It was in fact, Mr Swallow's grandfather who built the pub
of local stone in the 1830s.

It is a clean, pleasant and homely village pub with 2 bars.

Awliscombe

THE HONITON INN
Awliscombe, Honiton. Tel: Honiton 2554

Bass Charrington

Map reference number: 91
Situated on the A373 Honiton to Cullompton road, 2 miles north-west of
Honiton.

Car park. Coaches by invitation. Bed & breakfast available in 4 rooms all
with hot & cold water. Resident's lounge.

Keg beers and draught local rough cider available. Pasties, ploughmans,
sandwiches, soups and coffee served over the bar.

A typical village pub with 2 bars — one the traditional local bar, the other
a small attractive lounge. Collections of plates and Victorian domestic
pottery decorate the interior.

Awliscombe is a good centre for touring South Devon. It is only 10 miles
from the sea. Private shooting and fishing can be arranged from
The Honiton Inn.

Axminster

THE GEORGE HOTEL
Victoria Place, Axminster. Tel: Axminster 32209

Bass Charrington

Map reference number: 98
Situated in the centre of Axminster, 5 miles from Lyme Regis and
6 miles from Seaton.

Car park. Coaches by arrangement. Bed & breakfast and full board
available in 12 rooms all with hot & cold water, some with private bath.

Draught Worthington, Carling lager, Guinness and keg Brew XI, Bass
special and Toby bitter available. Basket meals, sandwiches, soups, salads,
paté and other hot snacks served over the bar. Table d'hôte and à la carte
menus served in the separate restaurant.

A coaching inn of the 18th century, *The George* is a solid stone, 3
storeyed building with a colour washed front. The archway, leading to the
courtyard, is the major entrance. Cromwell's troops were billeted at the
hotel when the Lyme Regis Roundheads beseiged the Cavaliers in the
church. Lord Nelson also stayed at *The George* on 15th January 1801.

THE HARBOUR INN
Axmouth, Nr Seaton. Tel: Seaton 20371

Free House

Map reference number: 97
Situated in Axmouth, 1 mile from Seaton, 5 miles from the
Dorset border.

Car park. Coaches by invitation. Lawn garden. Children's room.

Worthington E from the wood, keg Double Diamond, Whitbread Tankard,
Youngers Tartan and lager, mead and parsnip wine available. Wide range of
snacks served over the bar. Full meals served in the separate restaurant.

A 12th century thatched building of stone, *The Harbour Inn* stands at the
beginning of the great Fosse Way and on the site of an important Roman
port. Axmouth is in fact one of the country's oldest villages.

The interior, with its original beams, great open fireplace, dark wood
furniture and antiques, maintains a pleasant old world atmosphere. The
burning of the Ashen Faggot on Christmas Eve is an historic annual
occasion. The gardens of *The Harbour* are always a delight.

TOBY JUG INN
Bickington, Nr Newton Abbot. Tel: Bickington 278

Heavitree

Map reference number: 103
Situated between Exeter and Plymouth on the A38,
7 miles from Newton Abbot and 11 miles from Torquay.

Car park. Coaches by appointment. Garden.

Range of draught and keg beers available. Pasties, cheese & onion, chicken
& mushroom pies, ploughmans and sandwiches served over the bar. The
fresh crab sandwiches are highly recommended.

An early 18th century building of cobb and stone the *Toby Jug* has an
attractive frontage. There are 2 bars.

Originally called the *Jolly Sailor Inn,* the pub's name was changed to
Toby Jug at the request of the landlords. They did this because of their
large collection of toby jugs gathered from all over the world — a collection that is growing still. At present it numbers about 220.

You wouldn't think there was enough room — but the pub also has on
display many hundreds of horse brasses and old muskets, guns and
swords.

With so many items to stimulate conversation the *Toby Jug* is sought out
by visitors and locals alike.

Bickleigh

THE FISHERMANS COT

Bickleigh, Nr Tiverton.   Tel: Bickleigh 237

Free House

Map reference number: 64
Stiuated beside Bickleigh Bridge in Bickleigh off the A396.
4 miles from Tiverton, 10 miles from Exeter.

Car park. Coaches by invitation. Riverside gardens. Children's room. Bed
& breakfast available in 6 double and 2 single rooms, all with hot & cold
water. 3 bathrooms en suite.

Draught Bass, keg Worthington E, Toby bitter, Whitbread Tankard, Brew
XI, Black Label and Guinness available. Grills, salads and snacks served over
the bar. Roasts, omelettes, grills and other special dishes served in the
separate restaurant.

An attractive and quaint thatched building, *The Fisherman's Cot* has 2 bars
both with an intimate and homely atmosphere. Open log fire burns in the
lounge. Singalongs are held on alternative Sunday evenings, and dinner/
dances every Friday and Saturday.

Bideford

NEW INN HOTEL

The Market Square, Bideford. Tel: Bideford 2810

Free House

Map reference number: 4
Situated in the centre of Bideford in North Devon on the estuary of the
River Torridge.

Car parking in town. Coaches by invitation. Bed & breakfast and full
board available in 28 rooms all with hot & cold water.

Wide selection of draught and keg beers available. Ploughmans, scampi
& chips, chicken & chips, salads and curries served over the bar. Luncheons
and dinners served in the separate restaurant.

The *New Inn* is over 500 years old, having been built as a coaching stage,
and is closely connected with Bideford's romantic history. The inn was
completely reconstructed in 1843, and refurnished in 1974, both in keeping with the original design.

The 2 bars are very comfortable and the service extremely good. There are
log fires and exposed beams. Families are very welcome.

CHICHESTER ARMS

Bishop's Tawton, Barnstaple. Tel: Barnstaple 3945

Watney Mann

Map reference number: 17
Situated just off the main Barnstaple to Exeter road, 2 miles from
Barnstaple.

Car park.

Keg Watney beers and 'Sidney's Special' available. Comprehensive range
of snacks and meals served over the bar.

The *Chichester Arms* is a very picturesque, cobb and thatch 15th century
inn. Set in the small, quiet village of Bishop's Tawton, the coat of arms of
the Chichester family hangs above the front door.

The interior has an old world atmosphere and décor. There are exposed
beams and a fine collection of brasses, antique guns and swords.

Blackawton

NORMANDY ARMS
Blackawton, Nr Dartmouth. Tel: Blackawton 316

Free House

Map reference number: 37
Situated 5 miles to the west of Dartmouth in the village of Blackawton.
9 miles from Totnes.

Car park. Coaches welcome. Lawn garden. Bed & breakfast available in 3
double rooms, 1 with private bath, and 1 single room.

Draught Bass, keg Watney special, Tartan, Tankard, mild, Worthington E,
Toby bitter, Carlsberg Hof, Carling Black label and rough cider available.
Snacks, scampi, pasties, salads and sandwiches served over the bar. A la
carte dinners served in the separate restaurant.

Situated on the side of a hill, the *Normandy Arms* is a 15th century village
pub, constructed of cobb and painted black on white. Sir Walter Raleigh was
married in the local village church.

Both bars have open log fires. The comfortable, olde worlde lounge is
decorated with momentoes of the 2nd World War. Darts can be played in
the Public Bar.

Bow Bridge

WATERMAN'S ARMS
Bow Bridge, Ashprington, Nr Totnes. Tel: Harbertonford 214

Free House

Map reference number: 39
Situated adjacent to Bow Bridge on the banks of the River Harbourne,
2½ miles from Totnes.

Car park. River bank for a garden. Children's room.

Keg Whitbread Tankard, Younger's Tartan, Double Diamond, Worthington
E, Skol lager, draught Guinness and very local cider available. Wide variety
of hot and cold dishes, including sandwiches, ploughmans, soups, paté,
salads, sweets served over the bar. Bread baked on the premises. Steaks,
fish, poultry, salads served in the separate restaurant. Egon Ronay
recommended.

The *Waterman's Arms* is situated at Bow Bridge which is recorded in the
Doomsday Book (1086), and until recently served as the local smithy. It is
an attractive 2-storey cobb and stone building.

Bowd

THE BOWD INN
Bowd, Nr Sidmouth. Tel: Sidmouth 3328

Devenish

Map reference number: 86
Situated 2 miles north of Sidmouth on the main A3052 Exeter to Seaton road,
at the junction of the Ottery St Mary road.

Car park. Coaches by invitation. Large garden. Bed & breakfast and full
board available in 5 rooms all with hot & cold water.

Devenish draught and keg beers, Whitbread Tankard, Heineken and draught
Guinness available. Soups, paté, basket meals, pies, sandwiches served over
the bar. A la carte menu, and table d'hôte luncheons served in the separate
restaurant. Seats 50. Egon Ronay recommended.

Housed in a genuine 12th century building, *The Bowd* opened as an inn in
1651. It is of wattle and cobb construction with a thatch roof. Extensive
alterations were carried out in 1974, and these were so skilfully executed
that conservationists have been generous in their praise.

The one large bar has a 12th century fireplace, where logs burn from
October to May. The walls and numerous exposed beams are decorated
with smugglers wooden kegs and a large collection of brass and copper.

The Bowd is situated in picturesque countryside in a valley between two
beauty spots, Bulverton Hill and Fire Beacon Hill. The name Bowd
originates from the Roman word Bowdena, meaning 'under the hill'.
In previous centuries the inn was used extensively by smugglers and free
traders, being only 2 miles from the sea.

Branscombe

YE OLDE MASONS ARMS

Branscombe, Nr Seaton.   Tel: Branscombe 300

Free House

Map reference number: **104**
Situated 1½ miles off the A35, 6 miles from Sidmouth and 4 miles
from Seaton.

Car park. Small garden with chairs. Bed & breakfast and half board
available in 19 rooms, all with hot & cold water, 12 with private
bathrooms.

Draught Devenish, Worthington E, keg Tankard, Trophy, Double Diamond
and Heineken lager. Wide range of snacks served over the bar. Excellent
meals available in the separate restaurant. Egon Ronay and Ashley
Courtenay recommended.

Built in the 14th century, this pub is constructed of stone and cobb with a
slate roof and thatched porches. *Ye Olde Masons Arms* is set at the coastal
end of Branscombe, a village of preserved beauty and great historic interest.
Fabulous stories are told of the Branscombe smugglers and the meetings
which took place at this ancient inn.

The interior has been restored recently to include every modern convenience,
but it retains its old world charm and character. There are plenty of
exposed beams in all the public rooms, and there are 3 open log fires.

Branscombe is well situated for tours of south Devon and for swimming.

Brixham

THE NEW QUAY INN
King Street, Brixham.   Tel: Brixham 2572

Courage

Map reference number: 76
Situated 50 yards from the harbour at Brixham.

Parking in the town. Coaches welcome. Bed & breakfast available in 4 double rooms, all with hot & cold water.

Keg Tavern, John Courage, mild, Guinness and Harp lager available. Grills, steaks, fish, basket meals, pizzas, sandwiches and ploughmans served in all bars.

Approximately 400 years old, *The New Quay* — also known as *The Hole in the Wall* — has witnessed many historic events. These include the landing by Sir Francis Drake of the first Spanish warship ever captured, and the arrival of William of Orange in 1688.

Thick stone walls, exposed low beams, and a smuggling history make this a super old-fashioned pub with a terrific atmosphere. An unusual collection of paper currency from all over the world decorates the walls.

Buckfastleigh

COTT ORCHARD INN
Totnes Road, Buckfastleigh, Nr Totnes. Tel: Buckfastleigh 2214

Free House

Map reference number: 46
Situated 1 mile from Buckfastleigh on the A384 to Totnes, a few yards off the new A38.

Car park. Coaches by appointment. Large garden with flowers, shrubs and trees.

Whitbread and Bass beers, and local cider available. Snacks and hot meals served over the bar. Table d'hôte and à la carte menus available in the separate restaurant.

Old English cottage style building with black and white frontage and attractive surroundings. The olde worlde interior, with its exposed beams and log fires, complements the exterior.

Local attractions include the Dart Valley Railway and Buckfast Abbey.

COACH AND HORSES
Buckland Brewer, Nr Bideford. Tel: Horns Cross 395

Free House

Map reference number: 3
Situated in Buckland Brewer village 7 miles south of Bideford.

Car park. Coaches by invitation. Very pretty beer garden. Children's room.
Bed & breakfast and full board available.

Keg Tankard, Worthington E, special, Trophy, Ben Truman and lager
available. Sandwiches, pies, ploughmans, basket meals and paté served over
the bar. Full à la carte menu served in the separate restaurant.

Steeped in history the *Coach and Horses* is a 13th century inn which has
retained much of its old world character and charm. Originally a coaching
stop between Barnstaple, many of the early settlers on their way to America
sought shelter here in the 1600s.

The *Coach & Horses* was also used as a courthouse in the 17th and 18th
centuries. Prisoners awaiting trial were strapped by their wrists to the low
oak beams. It is even said that executions were carried out here.

The oak beams, thatched roof, open stone fireplace and original bread
oven have all been preserved. The inn is situated in some of the most beautiful scenery in the west country.

Burgh Island

PILCHARD INN

Burgh Island, Bigbury-on-Sea, Nr Kingsbridge. Tel: Bigbury-on-Sea 344

Free House

Map reference number: 34
Situated on Burgh Island which is 300 yards offshore from Bigbury-on-Sea.
8 miles from Kingsbridge, 20 miles from Plymouth.

Car park on mainland. Coaches welcome by invitation. 20 acres of garden.
Accommodation available in 35 self-catering rooms, all with kitchenettes
and bathrooms, in the Aparthotel. Evening dinner included. Children
welcome.

Wide range of keg beers and draught cider available. Ploughmans, soups,
salads and cold snacks served over the bar. Substantial 4-course home-
cooked dinners served in the Aparthotel restaurant.

Built in 1336 the *Pilchard* was originally used as a monk's rest house.
Later the island became a smuggler's paradise and this inn an ideal refuge.
It is said that Tom Crocker, the pirate, had his headquarters here. The sign
of the skull and cross-bones still hanging bears witness to this period.

The 3 bars are old, unspoilt and friendly. Log fires burn in winter. When
the tide is out visitors can walk to the island. At high tide transport to the
island is available by means of a unique sea tractor.

Cadeleigh

CADELEIGH ARMS INN

Cadeleigh, Tiverton. Tel: Bickleigh 238

Free House

Map reference number: 63
Situated 1 mile from Bickleigh and the Exe Valley and 4 miles from
Tiverton.

Car park. Coaches by invitation. Beer garden. Bed & breakfast and full
board available in 3 rooms all with hot & cold water.

Double Diamond, John Courage, Youngers Tartan, Starlight, Tankard,
Worthington E, Carlsberg lager, Alexander brandy and Cornish mead
available. Sandwiches, salads and ploughmans served in the separate
restaurant. Texas T-bone and New York Strip Steaks are the specialities
of the house.

The *Cadeleigh Arms* stands on the site of a 12th century building. It is
built principally of stone, and has 2 bay windows. There are stone granite
inglenook fireplaces in both bars and exposed beams in the restaurant.

Folk singing and other live music played in the pub.

Chagford

RING O'BELLS

The Square, Chagford. Tel: Chagford 2466

Free House

Map reference number: 53
Situated in the centre of Chagford village, 5 miles east of
Moretonhampstead on Dartmoor.

Coaches welcome. Beer garden. Bed & breakfast available in 4 double
rooms all with hot & cold water.

Keg Double Diamond, Worthington E, Tankard, Ben Truman, Trophy and
Carlsberg Hof lager available. Large range of snacks served over the bar.
Full a la carte menu served in the separate restaurant.

The *Ring O'Bells* is situated in one of the prettiest villages in Devon. Dating
back from about 1170 this inn has always been the centre of village
activities. It is the meeting place for the mid-Devon hunt.

The oak panelling, beamed ceiling, stone fireplaces and carved oak bar
combine to create a charming old world interior. The atmosphere is relaxed
and friendly.

Chardstock

THE GEORGE
Chardstock, Nr Axminster. Tel: South Chard 241

Watney Mann

Map reference number: 99
Situated 1 mile west of the Chard to Axminster road in the old village
of Chardstock. 5 miles north of Axminster.

Car park. Coaches welcome. Large lawn and cobbled yard with stabling
facilities. Bed & breakfast available in 4 double rooms, 3 with hot & cold
water.

Keg and bottled Watney beers available. Sandwiches and ploughmans
served over the bar.

The George, built in the 11th century, was originally the church. Linen-
fold panelling, low ceilings and staircase used in the church can still be seen.
It is an attractive low, thatched building painted white.

The one bar is local, friendly and old world with lots of brass ornaments
on display.

Cheriton Fitzpaine

RING OF BELLS
Cheriton Fitzpaine, Nr Crediton. Tel: Cheriton Fitzpaine 374

Free House

Map reference number: 65
Situated 1½miles west off the A3072, 5 miles north-east of
Crediton and 8 miles from Tiverton.

Car park. Coaches by invitation. Bed & breakfast and full board
available in 3 double rooms, 1 with bath en suite and 1 single
room. All with hot & cold water and shaver points.

Keg Whitbread, Watney, Ind Coope beers and Carlsberg Hof lager available.
Hot and cold snacks served over the bar. Meals to order.

A 14th century 2-storey thatched building of stone and cobb, the *Ring of
Bells* was probably used as the local church house or hostel. The one bar is
comfortably old world with low ceilings and exposed beams.

Cheriton Bishop

THE OLD THATCH
Cheriton Bishop, Nr Exeter. Tel: Cheriton Bishop 204

Free House

Map reference number: 57
Situated on the main A30, 10 miles from Exeter and 13 miles from
Okehampton.

Car park opposite.

Courage best bitter from the wood, draught Whitbread Tankard, Worthington E, Double Diamond, Alpine Ayingerbrau lager, Carlsberg Hof lager,
and a comprehensive range of bottled beers and lagers available. Mead and
Devon Farmhouse cider also served.

Food is served over the bar at lunchtimes only. In summer a cold table is
available and in winter home-made pies, 'Thatchers' lunch, soups, home-
made paté. Full à la carte menu, including flambé dishes, served in the
separate restaurant.

Originally a 16th century staging post on the London-Penzance run,
The Old Thatch is an attractive thatched, low cottage-style building.
Rough rendered and painted white over cobb walls it stands on the edge of
Dartmoor National Park. The one bar is extremely comfortable, furnished
with settles made by a local craftsman. It has exposed beams and a
traditional Devon inglenook fireplace with granite pillars.

The restaurant is worthy of special mention as the standard of cuisine
and service is very high. Vegetables and meat are purchased fresh daily,
and the proprietors prepare all dishes themselves.

It is hoped to make hand-bell ringing a regular feature in the future.

Chittlehamholt

THE EXETER INN
Chittlehamholt, Umberleigh.   Tel: Chittlehamholt 281

Free House

Map reference number: 22
Situated east off the main A377 Barnstaple to Exeter road, 5 miles from
South Molton and 12 miles from Barnstaple.

Car park. Coaches welcome. Open paddock garden. Bed & breakfast available in 3 double rooms, 2 with hot & cold water.

Keg Watney special, Starlight, Whitbread Tankard, Trophy, Double Diamond,
Guinness, Carlsberg Hof lager, 21 bottled beers and extra dry draught cider
available. Sandwiches, ploughmans, pasties, basket meals served over the bar.

A 400 year old, thatched village inn built of stone and cobb, *The Exeter* is
set in glorious Devon countryside. It was originally a carrier's house and
badger baiting is recorded as having taken place here.

The single bar, served by a central servery, is comfortable and friendly.
There are open log fires, exposed beams, inglenook fireplace with bread
oven and a collection of brass and copper ornaments. Darts matches and
sing-songs are the only functions held in the pub.

Chudleigh

THE OLD COACHING HOUSE
Chudleigh, Nr Newton Abbot.   Tel: Chudleigh 853270

Free House

Map reference number: 68
Situated in the centre of Chudleigh, a village east of the main A38 Plymouth to Exeter road. 5 miles from Newton Abbot, 9 miles from Exeter.

Car park. Coaches welcome.

Keg Whitbread Tankard, Trophy, mild, Worthington E, Double Diamond
and Stella Artois and Heineken lagers available. Comprehensive range of
salads, sandwiches, toasties, sweets served over the bar. A la carte menu of
grills served in the separate restaurant.

The main part of this inn is Georgian, being one of the buildings in an
entire street rebuilt after a fire in 1804. Other parts date from the 17th
century. Originally a staging post on the London to Plymouth route, *The
Old Coaching House* has offered its hospitality to royalty, including King
William IV and William of Orange.

Chudleigh Knighton

CLAYCUTTERS ARMS
Chudleigh Knighton, Nr Bovey Tracey. Tel: Chudleigh 3345

Heavitree

Map reference number: 70
Situated in the village of Chudleigh Knighton, 2 miles from Bovey
Tracey and 6 miles from Newton Abbot.

Car park. Coaches welcome. Garden and orchard. Bed & breakfast
with evening meals, available in chalets with showers.

Draught Worthington E, Trophy, Guinness, keg Tankard, Heineken,
cider, mild, mead, parsnip and blackcurrant wines available. Range of
snacks served over the bar.

This inn is named after the local industry, that previously flourished —
china clayworks. *The Claycutters* was converted from a row of thatched
cottages originally built in the 17th century. Charles I is reputed to have
stayed here whilst reviewing his troops in the area.

The bar has exposed beams, open fireplaces, a circular staircase and old salt
cupboards. The ghost of an unknown old lady is said to haunt the pub.

Chulmleigh

THE BARNSTAPLE INN
South Molton Street, Chulmleigh. Tel: Chulmleigh 388

Watney Mann

Map reference number: 24
Situated off the main A377 Exeter to Barnstaple road, 16 miles from
Barnstaple and 15 miles from Okehampton.

Parking in street. Bed & breakfast available.

Draught and bottled Watney beers and Devonshire cider available. Basket
meals of scampi, steak and chicken, soups, rolls and snacks served over
the bar.

The Barnstaple dates from 1633 and is a fine example of the coaching
inns of the period. The inn also served as a courthouse. It is believed that
the cut-away sections in the low oak beams of the main bars were made
to enable helmetted guards to stand upright during court sessions.

Charles I is reputed to have stayed here in 1644 while on a tour in the
first wheeled carriage. The Royal Coat-of-Arms is preserved over the fireplace in one of the guest bedrooms.

CAT & FIDDLE INN
Sidmouth Road, Clyst St Mary, Exeter. Tel: Topsham 3317

Whitbreads

Map reference number: 81
Situated on the main road in Clyst St Mary, 6 miles from Exeter.

Car park. Coaches welcome. Large lawn garden. Children's room.
Holiday caravans to let.

Keg Tankard bitter and Heineken lager available. Snacks served over the
bar.

A black & white timber and stone low period building, the *Cat & Fiddle*
was constructed in the 14th century. It was used extensively by smugglers
in earlier centuries.

The bars are decorated with interesting old blacksmiths tools, metal pieces
and bits. The furniture is period in keeping with the pub's age. The East
Devon hunt meet here several times every season.

There is a large camping and touring van park by the pub with full
facilities.

THE DRUM INN

Cockington, Torquay. Tel: Torquay 65143

Ind Coope

Map reference number: 74
Situated in the picturesque, unspoilt village of Cockington 2 miles from
Torquay and ¾ mile from the sea-front.

Car park. Fully landscaped garden. Children's room with games.

Draught and keg Ind Coope beers, country style wines and special cider
cups available. Full range of snacks served over the bar. Coffee, Devon
cream teas, lunch menu served in separate restaurant.

Built in 1935 *The Drum* was designed by Sir Edward Lutyens to blend
with the village of Cockington. It has faced brick walls and a thatched roof.
Some walls of the restaurant are 600 years old, having been part of 'Home
Farm' that previously stood on the site. A water wheel stands at the side of
the restaurant. It used to power a saw mill. It is said that *The Drum* is so
called because it stands on the spot where a drummer boy was killed during
a local uprising.

There are 3 bars. One has exposed beams and is decorated with old farm
implements, gin traps, badger trap, knives and a man trap. Another bar
has been decorated with a naval theme.

All the buildings in Cockington village are thatched and unspoilt — the forge
is known all over the world for its tiny lucky horseshoes.

Cockwood

THE SHIP INN
Cockwood, Starcross, Nr Exeter. Tel: Starcross 373

Courage

Map reference number: 78
Situated on the A376 coast road from Exeter to Dawlish, 8 miles from
Exeter, 3 miles from Dawlish.

Car park. Coaches by arrangement. 2 beer gardens. Children's room.

Draught & keg Courage bitters, draught Guinness and Harp lager,
bottled beers and mead available. Wide range of snacks and meals,
including local seafood dishes, served over the bar. Delicious at reasonable
prices.

The Ship, originally an old victualler's house, dates from 1640 and is built
of cobb. Old ovens can be seen in the Lounge Bar — one recently uncovered
and believed to be over 450 years old. These ovens were extensively used
in the days when the river estuary ran by the inn, and when sailors obtained
all their provisions here. The coming of the railway closed the entrance to
the inlet.

Coleford

THE NEW INN
Coleford, Nr Crediton.   Tel: Copplestone 242

Free House

Map reference number: 59
Situated 2 miles off the A377 Crediton to Barnstaple road, 4 miles from
Crediton.

Car park. Coaches by appointment.

Draught Whitbread best bitter, keg Youngers Tartan, Whitbread Tankard,
Worthington E, Guinness, Heineken lager and local draught cider available.
Chicken, scampi, scallops basket meals, toasted & plain sandwiches,
ploughmans and salads served over the bar.

Situated in the picture postcard village of Coleford which is designated as a
conservation area, the 13th century stone, cobb and thatch *New Inn* is itself
listed as a building of historic importance and of architectural interest.

All 3 inter-connecting bars have a super old world atmosphere. They are
furnished with antique settles and brass and copper ornaments. There are
many exposed beams and 2 large open fires.

Combe Martin

PACK OF CARDS

High Street, Combe Martin, Ilfracombe. Tel: Combe Martin 3327

Free House

Map reference number:19
Situated in the centre of Combe Martin, 10 miles from Ilfracombe.

Large car park. Coaches by invitation. Lawn garden between the pub and a stream is a great attraction in fine weather.

Variety of keg beers available. Soup, ploughmans and paté served over the bar. Home-made light food available in the Pub Grub and Wine Room up-stairs.

This unusual 17th-century building was constructed by the then local squire, George Ley, to commemorate his luck at cards. It represents a pack of cards — the 4 floors are the 4 suits each with 13 doors, and 52 windows represent each individual card. Some windows were later blocked in to avoid window tax. George Ley died in 1716 and the house became an inn.

Pack of Cards has 3 bars, Public, Lounge and Smoke Room. The Pub Grub room has a superb ceiling and an open fire. A curiosity not to miss is the press gang table, which concealed 3 men whenever the abductors were searching the inn for volunteer sailors.

Folk singing and guitar music.

Dalwood

TUCKERS ARMS
Dalwood, Nr Axminster.   Tel: Stockland 342

Bass Charrington

Map reference number: 95
Situated in Dalwood, 4½ miles from Axminster and 6 miles from
Honiton.

Car park. Coaches welcome. Large lawn and beer garden. Skittle alley where
children are admitted.

Draught and keg Bass beers available. Wide variety of snacks served over the
bar.

Situated 2 miles off the main road, the *Tuckers Arms* was built in the 12th
century to house the workmen who constructed the local church. The church
is one of the oldest in Devon. The *Tuckers* is built of cobb and is very
attractive with a thatched roof. The building is held under a preservation
order.

The interior has a fine old stone and slate floor, inglenook fireplace with
bread oven and a good, friendly atmosphere. The old-fashioned game of
skittles, with heavy balls on a hard long alley, is played here. Skittle parties
are catered for.

The Ashen Faggot is burnt here every Halloween, Christmas Eve and New
Years Eve. Piano music is played in the bar every Saturday from June until
September.

Dartington

THE COTT INN

Dartington, Nr Totnes.   Tel: Totnes 863777

Free House

Map reference number: 42
Situated in the village of Dartington 1½ miles from Totnes.

Car park. Coaches by invitation. Lawn garden. Patio at front. Bed & breakfast available in 6 rooms all with hot & cold water.

Double Diamond, Worthington E, Ben Truman, Whitbread Tankard and
Ansell's mild available. Full range of bar snacks. Table d'hôte and à la carte
menus served in the separate restaurant.

The Cott is said to have been named after Johannes Cott, who became a
freeman of Totnes in 1333, and who used the original cottages as a change
house for his pack horses. Built of cobb and stone, this inn has an extremely attractive low, thatched profile.

Cock-fighting took place here and vast sums of money changed hands. Cider
was also brewed and sold for as little as ½d per gallon. Inspired by *The
Cott's* atmosphere and its surrounding countryside, Daniel Defoe, so it is
said, wrote *Robinson Crusoe* here.

The long, period bars are comfortable and attractive with low timbered
ceilings and panelled bars.

This inn is within easy reach of Dartmoor, the sea, Dartington Hall, and
the River Dart. Riding, fishing, sailing, walking are all available close by.

Dartmouth

THE CHERUB
13 Higher Street, Dartmouth. Tel: Dartmouth 2571

Free House

Map reference number: 38
Situated in central Dartmouth, 3 minutes walk from the lower ferry.

Parking available in town.

Keg Worthington E, Double Diamond, Tartan, Tankard, Carlsberg
Export lager and Guinness available. Home-made paté, French onion soup,
cottage pie, fresh crab, ravioli, salads, sandwiches and ploughmans served
over the bar.

The Cherub is the oldest house in the historic seafaring town of Dartmouth.
Built originally as a wool-merchants house, the pub derived its name from a
type of schooner — Cherub — built on the Dart for exporting wool and wine.
It was constructed around 1380 of old oak timbers, 90% of which are still
the original. The type of beam construction is most unusual and is known as
Dragon beaming. All beams are exposed inside and out.

There are 2 bars joined by an old twisting staircase. The restoration of the
interior, completed in 1958, was done very tastefully. All the furniture and
settles were specially made locally at Dartington Hall. Windows on the first
floor are the originals, uncovered during the restoration, and are of a type
not previously seen.

Dartmouth

RALEIGH HOTEL
South Embankment, Dartmouth. Tel: Dartmouth 2360

Free House

Map reference number: 38
Situated in the centre of Dartmouth on the estuary.

Car park. Coaches by appointment. Bed & breakfast available in 36 rooms
all with hot & cold water.

Draught Tankard, Red Barrel, Worthington E, Double Diamond, Tartan,
M & B mild, Harp lager and cider available. Hot platters, sandwiches,
ploughmans and other snacks served over the bar. 3-course dinners
served in the separate restaurant.

Devonport

OLD CHAPEL
Cumberland Gardens, Devonport, Plymouth. Tel: Plymouth 51777

Watney Mann

Map reference number:101
Situated 2 miles from Plymouth centre on the Cornwall road.

Car park. Coaches by invitation. Paved area in front with tables and chairs.

Draught and keg Watney beers available. Hot and cold food served over the bar. Extensive menu, including steak and seafood, served in the separate restaurant.

Originally built as a Unitarian Chapel in 1790, its congregation remained small after dockyardsmen had been threatened with dismissal if they joined the new sect. This was because Unitarianism supported the French Revolution, a movement much hated in England. The chapel was converted in 1801 for the sale of alcohol.

This old quaint stone and cobb building — now protected — still retains remnants of its ecclestiastical character. There are 3 bars, all furnished in keeping with the age of the pub. One of the most unusual inns in the country.

Doddiscombsleigh

THE NOBODY INN
Doddiscombsleigh, Nr Exeter.   Tel: Christow 394

Free House

Map reference number: 67
Situated in the village, 2 miles west of the A38 Exeter to Plymouth road,
6 miles from Exeter.

Car park. Bed & breakfast and full board available in 4 rooms all with
showers and hand basins.

Whitbread Tankard, Toby, Bass special, Worthington E, Youngers Tartan,
Red Barrel, Carling Black Label, Carlsberg Hof, Guinness and Blackthorn
cider available. Over 60 whiskies, including malt whiskies from every area in
Scotland, also available. Snacks served over the bar. A la carte dinners
served in the separate restaurant.

A 16th century white-washed cobb inn, that has been cleverly put together
from farm cottages and outbuildings and enlarged. Originally called the
New Inn there are several explanations as to why the name was changed.

One is that there was a lazy landlord who seldom opened his door to
customers. Thus people thought there was nobody in. Another story
states that when a wake was in progress for the landlord of the *New Inn,*
a messenger rode from Exeter, shouting that the bearers had taken the
wrong coffin. The one they were carrying had nobody in it.

The interior has low beams, open fires, antique furniture and its walls are
decorated with old prints, pictures and brass pieces.

Drewsteignton

DREWE ARMS
Drewsteignton, Nr Moretonhampstead.   Tel: Drewsteignton 224

Whitbreads

Map reference number: 55
Situated in Drewsteignton village, 1 mile south of the main A30 Exeter to
Okehampton Road.

Car park.

Whitbread beers and mead available. Sandwiches and ploughmans served
over the bar.

This is a charming, old world village pub, originally called the *Druids Arms.*
It has an attractive, low thatched profile and is situated next to the church
in the tiny village of Drewsteignton.

The interior is full of character.

SIR WALTER RALEIGH INN

East Budleigh, Nr Budleigh Salterton.   Tel: Budleigh Salterton 2510

Devenish

Map reference number: 85
Situated in the centre of the old village of East Budleigh, off the A376.
2 miles from Budleigh Salterton and 6 miles from Exmouth.

Car park.

Devenish draught and bottled beers, keg Whitbread and lager. Excellent hot
and cold snacks, with seafood a speciality, served over the bar.

A thatched 2-storey stone and cobb building, parts of which were built in
the 16th century. It is situated close to a 14th century church and only 1
mile from Hayes Barton, birthplace of the famous navitator and explorer —
Sir Walter Raleigh. Sir Walter's house is open to the public and the pub is
named after this well-known local.

The interior has a cosy atmosphere throughout. Both bars have low ceilings
with old beams and open fires.

East Prawle

PIG'S NOSE INN
East Prawle, Nr Kingsbridge. Tel: Chivelstone 209

Free House

Map reference number: 102
Situated at the most southerly point of Devon, south of the A379 Kings-
bridge to Dartmouth road. 9 miles from Kingsbridge and 15 miles from
Dartmouth.

Car parking on the village green. Coaches welcome.

Keg Whitbread Tankard, Red Barrel, Watney special bitter and mild,
Ushers, draught Guinness, Carlsberg lager and local draught sweet and dry
cider available. Ploughmans, quiches, sandwiches, paté, things with chips
and pasties served over the bar. Fresh local lobsters, Dover soles, steaks,
ducklings, home-grown vegetables served in the separate restaurant. Seats
16. Booking essential.

The building is of local stone and of a design typical in the South Hams
district 400 years ago. 100 years ago it was known as the *Union Inn* and
under that name it made a macabre mark in history.

On 4th December 1872 an Italian ship was wrecked on Prawle Point. The
survivors went to the *Union* for food and rest. They all retired early but
later the landlord was surprised to hear a disturbance from the sailors'
room. One of the sailors was threatening all-comers with a knife. He finally
broke out and ran amok through the village "spilling good Devon blood."
Happily such excitement rarely disturbs the village quiet.

The pub got its new name - *Pig's Nose* - from an unusual shaped rock
found off the coast of Prawle.

THE SHIP INN

Martins Lane, Exeter.   Tel: Exeter 72040

Whitbreads

Map reference number: 66
Situated in the well-known lane, linking Exeter High Street with the
Cathedral Close.

Draught Whitbread best, Trophy, Bass, Worthington E, Red Barrel,
Tankard, Heineken and Stella Artois lagers available. Filled baps,
sandwiches and hot snacks served over the bar. Rump. T-bone, fillet steaks,
gammon and fish served in the upstairs restaurant.

Built in the 16th century, *The Ship* was well patronised by famous Devon
men, including Francis Drake, Walter Raleigh and John Grenville.
During the Civil War the Cavalier, Captain Benet, quartered his men at
The Ship. Benet described it as "an excellent place with good wine, victuals
and forage and an upright man for host."

In 1710 a mob, angered by the trial of Dr Sacheverell who had preached
against the unpopular Whig Government of the day, tried to burn down
The Ship because they believed some Whig-sponsored clergy were hiding
there. Soldiers came out and, in the words of an eye-witness, "made an end
of the fire and very nigh of the rioters as well."

The interior is full of atmosphere, beams and customers.

Exeter

THE PROSPECT INN
The Quay Steps, Exeter. Tel: Exeter 73152

Heavitree

Map reference number: 66
Situated on the quayside in the city of Exeter.

Car park. Patio at the front.

Keg Tankard, Trophy, Worthington E, Bass, Heineken lager and draught
Guinness available. Wide range of snacks, including help yourself buffet
food, served over the bar.

Originally constructed in the 1700s, *The Prospect* is set on the old Exeter
quay with a Maritime Museum next door. Parts of the Onedin Line were
filmed here.

There are 2 bars - one lounge and one cocktail bar. Exposed beams are a
feature of both bars.

Boating and fishing available all year round. Sights of the city of Exeter
within walking distance.

Exeter

VICTORIA INN
Union Road, Exeter. Tel: Exeter 54176

Devenish

Map reference number: 66
Situated on the main route to the city centre. 15 minutes walk from
the main shopping centre.

Parking in road. Coaches by invitation. Bed & breakfast available in 3
double rooms, all with hot & cold water.

Draught and keg beers, Guinness, Tankard, Saxon, IPA, Heineken and
draught local cider. Salads, ploughmans, beefburgers, sandwiches and rolls
served over the bar.

Approximately 100 years old, the *Victoria* has a very Victorian appearance.
It is situated close to Exeter University, and every year the students
attempt to drink the pub dry of draught beer during rag week. They suc-
ceeded in 1972 and 1973 and plaques on the wall comemorate these :hese
successes. The *Victoria* is twinned with a student bar in Brest.

Exmouth

BUILDERS ARMS
Princes Street, Exmouth.   Tel: Exmouth 3858

Devenish

Map reference number: 84
Situated in Exmouth town centre, behind the Post Office.

Car parking in the town.

Devenish bitter, Whitbread Tankard, Saxon keg bitter, draught Guinness,
Heineken lager, mead, apple wine and rough cider available. Snacks served
over the bar.

A variety of carved heads are found on the outside of this building, which
are said to be connected with the beer brewed on the premises in earlier
days. Part of the friendly bar still has exposed beams.

Exmouth can offer a good beach, Zoo, river and fishing trips.

Fairmile

THE FAIRMILE INN
Fairmile, Nr Ottery St Mary.   Tel: Ottery St Mary 2827

Free House

Map reference number: 90
Situated on the A30 at Fairmile which is 1 mile from Ottery St Mary. 5 miles
from Honiton and 6 miles from Sidmouth.

Car park. Coaches by arrangement.

Draught Bass, keg Starlight, Double Diamond, Tartan, Tankard, Carling
Black Label, Guinness and wide variety of bottled beers available.
Soups, paté, sandwiches, ploughmans, pasties, pies, omelettes, chicken,
scampi, curry, sweets and coffee served over the bar. Excellent and distinctive food served in the separate restaurant. Seats 26.

Scheduled as a building of historic and architectural importance, it is
rectangular and regular in shape. Rendered, painted white and black,
with mock shutters, it is alleged to date from Cromwell's period. Cromwell
is said to have killed a Cavalier here and to have hung another from the
rafters.

There are 2 bars and a restaurant. All have low ceilings and open fireplaces.
The atmosphere is comfortable and welcoming.

Fingle Bridge

THE ANGLER'S REST

Fingle Bridge, Drewsteignton.   Tel: Drewsteignton 287

Free House

Map reference number: 56
Situated at the famous beauty spot of Fingle Bridge in Dartmoor National
Park, near to Drewsteignton, 2 miles from the A30 and 13 miles from
Exeter.

Car and coach parks. Coaches by appointment. Large terraced garden on
riverside, adjoining and overlooking Fingle Bridge. Children welcome in the
restaurant.

Worthington E, Courage best, Bass special bitters and local farm cider
available. Hot and cold snacks served over the bar. Morning coffee, lunches,
Devonshire cream teas and dinners served in the separate restaurant. Noted
for its Devonshire fare and recommended in *Gourmet.*

An attractive building constructed in 1957, and according to Dartmoor
National Park requirements in suitable colours and style with granite
features. *The Angler's Rest* is fully open from Easter to October, and on
Sundays, and for private functions, during the winter.

The interior décor and atmosphere in the one Poacher's Bar is highly
praised, being in keeping with this unique beauty spot. A large free-standing
granite fireplace dominates the bar, while trophy fish and fishing rods
decorate the walls.

R D Blackmore declared that Fingle Bridge was "the finest scene in all
England". It adjoins the National Trust property of Castle Drago.

Harberton

CHURCH HOUSE INN

Harberton, Nr Totnes.   Tel: Totnes 863707

Free House

Map reference number: 40
Situated ¾ mile from the A31 Totnes to Kingsbridge road. 2½ miles from
Totnes.

Car park. Bed & breakfast and half board available in 2 rooms.

Tankard, Trophy, Worthington E, M & B mild, Carlsberg lager and local
cider available. Range of snacks served over the bar. Meals to order, for 4 or
more, in the separate restaurant.

Built around 1100, when thatched roofs were the fashion, this inn was first
used as a charity house for the Monks. In 1327 the Abbot and Monks hand-
ed the house over to the poor. In June 1950 it finally passed out of the
hands of the Church.

Fluted beams of mellow oak, a fine complete oak screen, and a lattice
window in the lounge of hand-made glass have been all carefully restored.
Also on display are a Tudor window frame, hidden at the time of the
Window Tax, and an original map by Robert Morden, dated 1694, of the
Harberton area.

Hatherleigh

GEORGE HOTEL

Hatherleigh.   Tel: Hatherleigh 454

Free House

Map reference number: 8
Situated on the A386, 7½ miles north-west of Okehampton.

Car park. Coaches welcome, preferably by prior arrangement. Swimming
pool with garden. Bed & breakfast and full board available in 13 rooms,
all with hot & cold water.

Keg Whitbread Tankard, Courage, Double Diamond, Worthington E, Trophy
bitters available. Good choice of snacks, including chef specials, served
over the bar. Table d'hôte and à la carte meals served in the separate
restaurant.

The *George* dates from 1450 and was originally a monk's retreat. It later
became a coaching inn and the tracks of the latter-day carriages across the
cobbled courtyard can still be seen. The inn at one time had its own beer
brew-house.

Lynmouth 20
19 Combe Martin
ILFRACOMBE
5 Mortehoe
WOOLACOMBE
6 Heanton
BRAUNTON
BARNSTAPLE
18 Swimbridge
Bishop's Tawton 17
A39
21 South Molton
4 Bideford
CLOVELLY
2 Horns Cross
UMBERLEIGH
Knowstone 60
22 Chittlehamholt
Buckland Brewer 3
23 Kingsnympton
1 Welcombe
TORRINGTON
7 Little Torrington
24 Chulmleigh
A 377
BUDE
HOLSWORTHY
8 Hatherleigh
A3072
59 Coleford
16 Sampford Courtenay
A388
14 Okehampton
25 Spreyton
Tedburn St Mary 58
15 Sticklepath
Cheriton Bishop 57
South Zeal 26
56 Fingle Bridge
55 Drewsteignton
A30
Sandy Park 54
Chagford 53
52 Moretonhampstead
LAUNCESTON
Lydford 9
51 North Bovey
A 386
50 Postbridge
DARTMOOR
BOVEY TRACEY
49 Widecombe-in-the-Moor
TAVISTOCK
PRINCETOWN
Bickington 103
A384
Hexworthy 28
A 390
47 Ashburton
Horrabridge 10
Torbryan 45
YELVERTON
Holne 48
11 Meavy
Staverton 44
Buckfastleigh 46
Dartington 42
Littlehempston 43
South Brent 29
Lutton 13
CORNWOOD
Harberton 40
41
Totnes
12 Plymouth
Avonwick 30
ASHPRINGTON
Devonport 101
Bow Bridge 39
31 Modbury
Blackawton 37
Kingston 32
36 Aveton Gifford
Ringmore 33
BIGBURY-ON-SEA
Burgh Island 34
35 Kingsbridge
SALCOMBE
East Prawle 102

48

EXMOOR
N
P
75
Tiverton 62
61 Pennymoor
A396
Cadeleigh 63
CULLOMPTON
65 Cheriton Fitzpaine
64 Bickleigh
A373
Upottery 92
CHARD
CREWKERNE
Chardstock 99
Stockland 93
CREDITON
Awliscombe 91
95 Dalwood
Hawkchurch 100
A38
HONITON
94
Axminster 98
Fairmile 90
Wilmington
A35
Ottery St Mary 89
Kilmington 96
Exeter 66
81 Clyst St Mary
88 Sidbury
Bowd 86
97 Axmouth
LYME REGIS
SEATON
87 Sidford
104 Branscombe
Topsham 80
82 Woodbury
67 Doddiscombsleigh
SIDMOUTH
A379
83 Withycombe Raleigh
85 East Budleigh
Starcross 79
BUDLEIGH SALTERTON
84 Exmouth
68 Chudleigh
Cockwood 78
70 Chudleigh Knighton
69 Ideford
DAWLISH
A380
77 Holcombe
71 Kingsteignton
TEIGNMOUTH
72 Newton Abbot
A 381
IPPLEPEN
Cockington 74
73 Torquay
TORBAY
A 385
75 Paignton
76 Brixham
38 Dartmouth

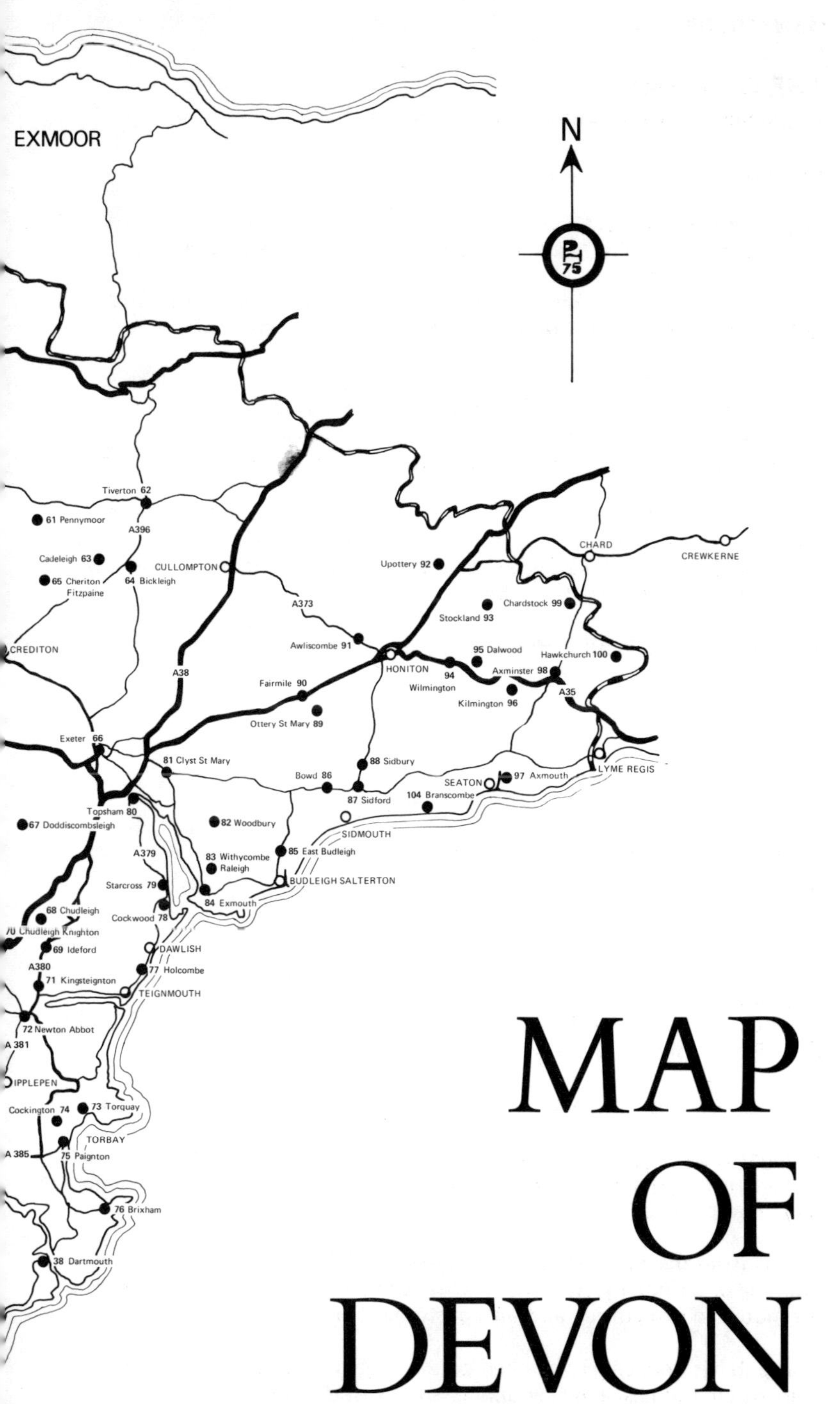

MAP

OF

DEVON

Hawkchurch

THE OLD INN
Hawkchurch, Nr Axminster.   Tel: Hawkchurch 309

Devenish

Map reference number: 100
Situated off the main Crewkerne road, 6 miles from Axminster.

Car park. Coaches by arrangement. Cobbled yard with tables for patron's use. Skittle alley. Bed & breakfast, with optional dinner, available in 4 rooms.

Draught and keg Devenish beers and Devon cider available. Wide selection of home-made pasties, basket meals, steaks and snacks served over the bar. Home-cooked meals, mainly grills, served in the separate restaurant.

Situated in the main street of Hawkchurch village opposite the church, *The Old Inn* was built in the 12th century. It was used by the masons who built the church and later became a Monastry. Some of the building was reconstructed in 1647 after a fire.

The inn has 2 bars both with a friendly, country trade. The regulars always make visitors feel at home.

Heanton

THE GIPSY MOTH
Braunton Road, Heanton, Nr Barnstaple. Tel: Braunton 813287

Free House

Map reference number: 6
Situated on the main A361 road between Barnstaple and Braunton. 2 miles from Barnstaple and 2 miles from Braunton.

Car park. Coaches welcome. Large lawn garden with children's play area.

Draught Worthington E, Black Label lager, mead and wide range of liquers and aperitifs available. Soup, patés, baps, sandwiches, sweets and ploughmans served over the bar.

Dating from the 17th century *The Gipsy Moth* is an alluring stone built building of baronial style with parapets and a Cornish slate roof. *The Moth* is reputed to be haunted and several stories abound as to its origins.

This pub has one, widely stocked bar decorated in Queen Anne style with high ornate ceilings, and fine upholstered period furniture.

Hexworthy

THE FOREST INN

Hexworthy, Nr Princetown, Dartmoor. Tel: Poundsgate 211

Free House

Map reference number: 28
Situated 1 mile off the main Ashburton to Tavistock road. 14 miles
from Tavistock and 9 miles from Ashburton.

Car park. Coaches by appointment. Lawn garden. Bed & breakfast
and full board available in 22 rooms, all with hot & cold water, some
with private baths.

Worthington E, Double Diamond, Red Barrel, Carlsberg and Carling Black
Label lagers available. Varied snacks from ploughmans to scampi & chips
served over the bar. Table d'hôte and à la carte meals served in the
separate restaurant.

Built at the beginning of the century, *The Forest* is situated in the forest
of Dartmoor. It is an imposing building of Dartmoor granite, with a
comfortable and traditional interior. There are 2 bars.

The Forest has its own horses that can be hired by guests. Ponies for
trekking available 1 mile away.

Holcombe

SMUGGLERS INN

27 Teignmouth Road, Holcombe, Dawlish. Tel: Dawlish 2301

Courage

Map reference number: 77
Situated on the main Dawlish to Teignmouth road. ¾ mile from
Dawlish and 1½ miles from Teignmouth.

Car park. Coaches by invitation. Terrace overlooking the bar.

Courage best bitter, Tavern keg, draught JC, Guinness, special mild, Harp
lager, keg Blackthorn cider and full range of bottled beers and liquers
available. Full range of cold snacks, sandwiches and salads, specialising
in seafoods, served over the bar.

Typical mid-18th century building made of cobb with a slate roof. An
extra bar and terrace was added in the 1960s. It was the only bar in Devon
with a full stock of spirits during the 1939-45 war.

The Smugglers has 3 bars. The Lounge is panelled, old world with a curved
bar. The Public Bar leads out to the terrace and another overlooks the sea.

Holne

CHURCH HOUSE INN

Holne, Nr Newton Abbot.   Tel: Poundsgate 208

Free House

Map reference number: 48
Situated on the south-east edge of Dartmoor, 4½ miles from Ashburton,
3½ miles from Buckfastleigh and 12 miles from Newton Abbot.

Car park. Coaches by arrangement. Bed & breakfast, with optional evening
meals, available in 5 rooms all with hot & cold water, shaver points and
central heating.

Ind Coope Super Draught, best bitter, Worthington E, M & B, IPA,
keg Whitbread Tankard, Double Diamond, Guinness, Carling Black Label
lager and range of country wines. Basket and plate meals served over the
bar at lunchtimes and in the evenings. Dinners available in separate
restaurant by prior booking.

White pebble dash rendering, partly black beamed, leaded light windows and
3 feet thick Dartmoor granite walls are the prominent features of this 14th
century inn. Oliver Cromwell is said to have stayed here during the Battle of
Totnes, and stabled his horse ½ mile down the road at the old Tithe Barn.

The friendly lounge bar is beamed with an open log fireplace. A woodscreen
across part of the bar is believed to be very old, almost as old as the building
itself, and is carefully preserved. The second bar is tastefully decorated.

Horrabridge

THE LEAPING SALMON

Horrabridge, Nr Yelverton.   Tel: Yelverton 2939

Courage

Map reference number: 10
Situated in the village of Horrabridge, 4 miles from Tavistock and 10 miles
from Plymouth.

Car park. Coaches by invitation. Benches to the front of the pub.

Draught and keg Courage beers available. Basket meals, salads,
sandwiches, ploughmans, pasties and fresh salmon served over the bar.

This is a stone and beamed building constructed around 1678. It was
originally a beer bar in a miner's cottage, but was later extended through
the neighbouring buildings to become what it is today. *The Leaping
Salmon* is situated opposite a river with a real salmon's leap.

HOOPS INN

Horns Cross, Bideford.   Tel: Horns Cross 222

Free House

Map reference number: 2
Situated on the main A39 midway between Bideford and Clovelly, 5 miles from each.

Car park. Coaches by arrangement. Garden for residents. Bed & breakfast and full board available in 16 rooms, all with hot & cold water.

Whitbread Trophy, Tankard, Double Diamond and Heineken lager available. Good range and freshly prepared hot and cold snacks served over the bar. Extensive table d'hôte and à la carte menus served in the separate restaurant. Prepared under Cordon Bleu supervision. Egon Ronay recommended.

Believed to date from the 13th century the *Hoops* is the manifestation of the ideal dream of a typical old English country inn. It is a white-washed Devon cobb building sheltered under a local wheaten reed thatch and set in 10 acres of a small hamlet in open country, about 1 mile from the sea.

The *Hoops* was undoubtedly used regularly by Sir Richard Grenville, born a few miles away, Drake, Raleigh and Hawkins. All sponsored the Bill, passed in 1566, that called for the construction of nearby Hartland Quay.

One long, low bar for all has oak beams, granite walls, panelling and open log fires. The inn has one room with a 4-poster bed, and holds the old Lorna Doone stagecoach which for years was all but the only public transport across wild Exmoor.

Ideford

ROYAL OAK INN

Ideford, Chudleigh, Nr Newton Abbot.   Tel: Chudleigh 852274

Heavitree

Map reference number: 69
Situated in Ideford village, 3 miles from Dawlish and 3 miles from
Newton Abbot.

Car park. Open lawn garden. Horses and dogs welcome.

Worthington E, Trophy, mild, Tankard, Heineken, mead, local wine and
cider available. Sandwiches, salads and ploughmans served over the bar.

A protected 17th century thatched building of stone and cobb, the
Royal Oak's sign depicts a crown in oak sprigs. This sign depicts an oak
tree, planted outside the pub, in commemoration of William of Orange's
visit in 1688. He and his followers stayed in Ideford after landing in
Brixham. Another interesting fact is that around 1840 Elias Truman
brewed his own beer in this pub when he wasn't making shoes for the
villagers.

Kilmington

THE NEW INN

Kilmington, Nr Axminster.   Tel: Axminster 33376

Palmer

Map reference number: 96
Situated in Kilmington, 200 yds off the main Axminster-Honiton road.
2 miles from Axminster, 6 miles from Honiton.

Car park. Coaches by appointment. Lawn with chairs and umbrellas.
Bed & breakfast available in 2 double rooms.

IPA bitter from the wood, top pressure best bitter, draught Guinness
and range of bottled beers available. Recommended by CAMRA. Sandwiches, salads, ploughmans and pies served over the bar.

Set in a rural setting, with views of Axe Valley, *The New Inn* is a
thatched building 350 years old. It is a super country inn, with 2 friendly
bars, where visitors are always made welcome. Exposed beams and open
fire in the lounge.

6 skittle teams, attached to the pub, can be seen in action in the pub's alley
3 times a week. Darts are also played. Tennis courts, bowling green, putting
green, cricket square and old church are all within 10 minutes walk.

THE CRABSHELL INN

Embankment Road, Kingsbridge. Tel: Kingsbridge 2345

Free House

Map reference number: 35
Situated on the water's edge of the Salcombe — Kingsbridge estuary, off the A379.

Car park. Coaches by arrangement. Covered patio on the estuary. 30 rooms available in adjacent Motor Inn, all with private baths, balconies, kitchenettes and colour televisions.

Worthington E and cider from the wood. Keg Tankard, Double Diamond, Tartan, mild, Guinness, Carlsberg and Carling lager. Wide range of snacks served over the bar. A la carte meals served in the separate restaurant.

The Crabshell has a super position and outlook across the water. Part of the building is 17th century, and though the interior is not olde worldy it is extremely pleasant and comfortable. Log fires burn in winter.

Kingsbridge is an ideal centre for sailing, boating, bird-watching, golfing, fishing, swimming and walking.

Kingsbridge

KINGS ARMS HOTEL
Fore Street, Kingsbridge. Tel: Kingsbridge 2071

Free House

Map reference number: 35
Situated on the main A379 in the centre of Kingsbridge. 20 miles
from Dartmouth.

Car park. Coaches welcome. Bed & breakfast and full board
available in 16 rooms, 9 with private baths or showers. 4 rooms with 4-
poster beds.

Keg Whitbread Tankard, Worthington E, Double Diamond, Courage IPA,
Harp and Carlsberg lagers, Wadworths bitter from the wood, mead and
apple wine available. Fish, chicken, scampi, soup, pies and sandwiches
served over the bar. Wide range of à la carte dishes, including jugged hare
and steak & oyster pie, served in the separate restaurant.

The *Kings Arms* is a typical old English inn that has been the centre of social
life in the South Hams peninsula since 1775. It has a ghost — a bride that
looks for her husband who is said to have disappeared on their wedding night
at the hotel in 1798.

Kingsnympton

GROVE INN
Kingsnympton, Umberleigh. Tel: Chulmleigh 406

Whitbread

Map reference number: 23
Situated in the village of Kingsnympton, south of the main A377
Barnstaple to Exeter road. 4 miles from South Molton and 16 miles
from Barnstaple.

Parking in village. Coaches by invitation. Skittle alley. Bed & breakfast
with optional evening meal, available in 3 double and 2 single rooms.

Whitbread keg bitters and from the wood. Hot & cold snacks served over
the bar. Evening meals by arrangement in the separate restaurant.

A stone and thatch village pub set in Kingsnympton square. Devon
village atmosphere exists at all times in the 2 bars. There are stone
walls, exposed beams and open fires. Skittles and other games are
played here.

Kingsteignton

OLD RYDON INN
Kingsteignton, Nr Newton Abbot.   Tel: Newton Abbot 4626

Free House

Map reference number: 71
Situated at the back of Kingsteignton village, 2 miles from Newton
Abbot.

Car park. Coaches by arrangement. Walled old world garden. Bed &
breakfast and full board available in 3 rooms all with hot & cold water.

Wessex IPA, Wadworths Old Timer, Whitbread Tankard, Worthington E,
Viking lager available. Home-made paté, soups, pies, goulash, vension
and rabbit served over the bar. Full, distinguished à la carte menu served
in the separate restaurant. Highly recommended.

Of cobb and slate construction, the *Old Rydon* dates from Saxon times.
It was converted in 1300 to house the masons who were building the
village church.

All downstairs rooms are beamed and all have open log fires. It is totally
un-plasticised and has been restored using old materials.

Kingsteignton

PASSAGE HOUSE INN
Hackney, Kingsteignton, Nr Newton Abbot.   Tel: Newton Abbot 3243

Heavitree

Map reference number: 71
Situated on the bank of the River Teign, ¾ mile down a lane off the Newton
Abbot to Teignmouth road.

Car park. Large terrace with lawn.

Whitbread Tankard, Trophy, Worthington E, Bass, Guinness, Harp and
Heineken lagers and mead available. Home-made pies, stews, curries,
steaks, fish, salads, sandwiches and ploughmans served over the bar.
Poultry, fish and grills served in the separate restaurant.

The original building dates from 1761 but the site has been occupied by
an inn from Roman times. This is because a pre-Roman ford was situated
here giving priests access between Bishopsteignton and Torre Abbey.

The dining room is beamed, the lounge bar has a lofted ceiling and open
fires burn in both. The atmosphere is relaxed.

Kingston

THE DOLPHIN INN

Kingston, Nr Modbury.   Tel: Bigbury-on-Sea 314

Courage

Map reference number: 32
Situated beside the church in Kingston village 3 miles from Modbury and
15 miles from Plymouth.

Car park. Coaches welcome. Lawn and flower garden.

Courage draught best bitter, keg Tavern and Harp lager available. Basket
meals, sandwiches, fish, grills, steak, gammon and ploughmans served over
the bar. Cold meats and pies served in the Buttery. Starters, steaks,
duckling, omelettes, salads, sweets and coffee served in the separate
restaurant.

The Dolphin is one of the few pubs with a road running through the
middle of it. The deeds of the buildings date back to 1550 and 1580, and
while two cottages were converted into the main building, on the other side
of the road is the Tallet Bar, originally a hayloft. The cellar of the main
building was used by local fishermen to store their catches. Brought by
donkey from the beaches, the fish was collected for the market at least
twice a week.

The 3 bars are fully carpeted with stone walls, old beams, period settles
and wood panelling. There are open log fires in 2 bars. The atmosphere is
congenial.

The village of Kingston has many extremely old, thatched buildings. It is
situated in quiet, open country and only 1 mile away from Wonwell beach.

Knowstone

THE MASONS ARMS
Knowstone, South Molton.   Tel: Anstey Mills 231

Free House

Map reference number: 60
Situated 1½ miles from the main A361, 8 miles from South Molton and
8½ miles from Tiverton.

Car park. Coaches by invitation. Lawn gardens. Bed & breakfast and full
board available in 4 double rooms, all with hot & cold water.

Whitbread, Courage, Watney, Bass bitters, Double Diamond, keg Tankard,
Guinness, Stella Artois lager and full range of whiskies available. Large
selection of snacks served over the bar. Full meals, including spit roast duck,
also served.

Named after its builders and first occupants, *The Masons Arms* was used
while skilled craftsmen worked on the 12th century church opposite. It is
an attractive low thatched building of cobb.

The interior has open log fires, and exposed beams throughout, including
the bathrooms. The atmosphere is dignified and comfortable.

Littlehempston

PIG & WHISTLE
Littlehempston, Nr Totnes.   Tel: Totnes 863733

Free House

Map reference number: 43
Situated 2 miles north of Totnes on the A381 Newton Abbot road.

Car park. Coaches by appointment.

Wadworth bitter from the wood, keg Tankard, Double Diamond, Brew XI,
Worthington E, Tartan, Guinness, Carling and Carlsberg Export lager
available. Full range of snacks and grills served over the bar.

The main part of the bar was built over 400 years ago. The stone-work has
now been rendered. There is a pleasant informal atmosphere in the one
long bar. The walls are of the original stone-work and there are exposed
beams and 2 open fires.

The ghost of a monk is reputed to roam the pub in search of a lost lover
who used to serve at the inn.

Little Torrington

GRIBBLE INN
Little Torrington, Nr Torrington.   Tel: Torrington 2235

Free House

Map reference number: 7
Situated on the A386 Bideford to Okehampton road, 4 miles from
Torrington.

Car park. Coaches welcome. Children's room. Bed & breakfast available in
5 rooms all with hot & cold water.

Double Diamond, Tankard, Worthington E, Starlight, Trophy, mild and
Bulmers cider available. Basket meals, ploughmans and sandwiches served
over the bar. Full menu including soups, steaks, fish, Gribble special grill
also available.

An L-shaped building with an original 16th century coaching wing, and a
modern extension. Two explanations as to the origins of its name have been
put forward — the name Gribble was given to a species of fish long since
disappeared and there was a wealthy, landowning family called the Gribbles.
The connection between a fish, family and pub is not at all apparent.

Lutton

THE MOUNTAIN INN
Lutton, Cornwood, Nr Ivybridge.   Tel: Cornwood 247

Free House

Map reference number: 13
Situated 1 mile west of Cornwood, and north of the A38 Plymouth road.
9 miles from Plymouth.

Car park. Patio.

Draught Courage IPA, keg Whitbread Trophy, Tankard, best mild, Youngers
Tartan, Stella Artois, Alpine lager and Guinness available. Individual cottage
pies, steak & kidney pies, hot bread with various fillings, tasty soups and
sandwiches served in the Hole in the Wall bar. Dinner served in the pub
by prior arrangement.

Built in the late 18th century, this pub was named after Lord Mountain
the local squire. It is one of the smallest pubs in Devon and has the appearance of a village cottage. The view from the front of the inn overlooking
Dartmoor National Park and the River Phial is magnificent.

The general décor has an unspoilt, old world appearance with exposed
timbers and 3 open log fires, 2 of which are granite surrounded.

Lynmouth

RISING SUN HOTEL

Mars Hill, Lynmouth.   Tel: Lynton 3223

Free House

Map reference number: **20**
Situated immediately opposite Lynmouth harbour, 20 miles
from Barnstaple.

Parking in village. Bed & breakfast and full board available in 15 rooms, all
with hot & cold water.

Selection of draught and keg beers available. Fresh sandwiches, salads,
ploughmans, chicken & chips, scampi & chips served over the bar. Full
table d'hôte and à la carte menus served in the separate restaurant.

A 14th century 2-storeyed, thatched building, the *Rising Sun* is situated
at the mouth of the River Lyn overlooking the harbour. Formerly a
fisherman's cottage, and now a protected building, it is said that part of
Lorna Doone was written here and that the poet Shelley drank here with
his young bride.

The one bar is long, warm and friendly. It is oak panelled, has exposed beams
and the original 14th century fireplace. The dining room is also panelled.

Poets through the ages must have been inspired by the *Sun's* grand views
of the sea and surrounding hills. The peaceful and unspoilt atmosphere of
this famous fishing village can still be enjoyed by tourists today. Boat
trips, sea fishing, salmon & trout river fishing, swimming, sailing, putting
and tennis are all within easy reach.

Lydford

THE CASTLE INN
Lydford, Nr Okehampton.   Tel: Lydford 242

Free House

Map reference number: 9
Situated 1 mile off the A386 mid-way between Okehampton and
Tavistock.

Car park adjacent. Coaches by invitation. Large lawn garden. Bed & breakfast, with optional meals, available in 5 rooms all with hot & cold water,
shaver points and fresh flowers.

Draught Courage PB, Worthington E, Courage special mild, Harp lager, keg
Whitbread Tankard, Youngers Tartan, Double Diamond, mead, draught
sherries, draught cider and wide selection of malt whiskies available.

Home-made soups, patés, fresh sandwiches, ploughmans, pasties, basket
meals served over the bar. Buffet table also available in Foresters Bar
from 12 – 2 p.m. Full à la carte menu available in the evening. Highly
recommended.

Constructed probably between 1500 and 1550, *The Castle* is situated in
Lydford village, next to Lydford Castle, an old Stannary prison dating
from 1195. It is only 200 yards from the National Trust area of Lydford
Gorge and close to one of the loveliest parts of Dartmoor.

Lydford

THE DARTMOOR INN
Lydford, Nr Okehampton.   Tel: Lydford 221

Free House

Map reference number: 9
Situated half-way between Okehampton and Tavistock on the main A386.

Car park. Coaches by invitation. Patio. Bed & breakfast and full board
available in 1 family suite, 4 double rooms (2 with bathrooms en suite) and
1 single room.

Draught Whitbread best, Bass, Guinness, Stella Artois lager and keg
Whitbread Tankard, best mild, a non-alcoholic Dartmoor Paradise and
Sangria available. Full range of snacks served over the bar. Table d'hôte and
à la carte luncheon and dinner menus available in separate restaurant.

A low cottage style building, *The Dartmoor* has been constructed in stages
– the oldest parts date from the 15th century.

ROYAL OAK INN
Meavy, Nr Yelverton.   Tel: Yelverton 2944

Free House

Map reference number: 11
Situated 1½ miles from Yelverton and the Plymouth to Tavistock road.
12 miles from Plymouth.

Car parking on green.

Draught, keg, bottled beers and Farmhouse cider available. Full range
of snacks such as pasties and sandwiches served over the bar.

Originally built in the 15th century of stone and cobb, the *Royal Oak*
was a church house and was used as a resting place by monks on their way
from Tavistock to Buckfast. It was named, according to records, after the
oak planted nearby in King John's reign. The pub is delightfully situated
on the village green next to the church.

The building is now owned by the Parish Council, having been bought
from the Church in early 19th century. The landlord is a tenant and pays
rent to the Council.

There are 2 bars, both with unspoilt character and a friendly atmosphere.
The public bar has an open log fire with side seats and a slate floor. The
landlord plays the Hammond organ most evenings.

Morris dancing, bell-ringing festivals and Meavy Oak Fair take place on
the village green.

Modbury

THE EXETER INN

Church Street, Modbury, Nr Plymouth.   Tel: Modbury 239

Watney Mann

Map reference number: 31
Situated in the main street of Modbury, 12 miles from Plymouth.

Parking in town. Coaches by arrangement. Secluded, terraced garden.
Children's room. Bed & breakfast available in 1 double room with private
bath and 1 single with hot & cold water.

Keg Watney bitter, Worthington E and Carlsberg lager available. Wide range
of hot and cold meals, served over the bar. 5-course table d'hôte dinners
served in the separate restaurant. French cuisine. Seats 30.

The exact date of construction of *The Exeter* is not known but it is
believed to be over 500 years old. It is an attractive black and white, half-
timbered building with large bow windows.

The inn was the headquarters of the Royalist forces before the Battle of
Modbury in 1643. It was also used as a courthouse in the 17th century,
became a coaching stop in the 1800s and brewed Devon's famous white
ale until the 1890s.

The one, low-beamed cosy bar is extremely attractive and well furnished.
The small restaurant is well-known and admired.

WHITE HORSE INN

The Square, Moretonhampstead.   Tel: Moretonhampstead 242

Free House

Map reference number: 52
Situated in the centre of Moretonhampstead on Dartmoor, 12 miles from
Exeter and 12 miles from Princetown.

Parking in town. Coaches by arrangement. Patio. Children's room. Bed &
breakfast and full board available in 9 rooms, 3 with private bath, 6 with
hot & cold water.

Keg Tankard, Trophy, Bass special, Worthington E, lager, draught Guinness,
Double Diamond, mild, mead and Devon scrumpy cider available. Basket
meals, soups, steaks, salads, ploughmans and sandwiches served over the bar.
A la carte and table d'hôte menus available in the separate restaurant. Seats
40.

Established in 1632, the *White Horse* is an attractive square, black & white
building, with shutters at the windows. It is set in Moretonhampstead on
Dartmoor and close to many beauty spots.

The inn has one old English bar with exposed beams, bow windows and
brass ornaments. The *White Horse* has its own disco.

CHICHESTER ARMS

Mortehoe, Woolacombe. Tel: Woolacombe 411

Watney Mann

Map reference number: 5
Situated in the centre of Mortehoe at the top of the hill from Woolacombe.
It adjoins National Trust coastal walks. 6 miles from Ilfracombe.

Car park. Terrace at front of house with bench seats and tables. Bed &
breakfast available in 2 rooms both with hot & cold water.

Keg Watney beers, draught Carlsberg lager and cider available. Hot pasties,
meat pies, ploughmans and sandwiches served over the bar.

A white-washed, low building of uncertain date, the *Chichester Arms* has
an attractive, shuttered frontage. The walls are 2' thick. There are 2 bars.
The Public Bar has lots of local atmosphere and a very old fireplace where
log fires burn in the winter. The Lounge Bar is wood-panelled and comfortably furnished, with a large local stone fireplace.

During the winter skittles, darts and crib are played. 4 skittle teams are
attached to the pub. In summer the pub is very busy with holiday makers,
being the only pub in the area.

YE OLDE CIDER BAR
East Street, Newton Abbot.   Tel: Newton Abbot 4221

Free House

Map reference number: 72
Situated in East Street in the centre of Newton Abbot.

Parking in town. Coaches by arrangement. Small garden.

No beer, no spirits — sells only sweet, dry, medium, farm ciders from the wood, and a selection of locally made wines. Soups, pies, pasties and toasted sandwiches served over the bar.

This inn has a real old-fashioned pub character. The atmosphere in the one long, narrow bar is friendly and warm.

Ye Olde Cider Bar has its own club the Long Bar Cork Club, so called from the shape of the bar and from the cork which each member carries. Founded about 70 years ago, Court sessions are held every Sunday when members tell tales on each other and are fined for their misdemeanours. This light-hearted fun provides entertainment for customers and easy money for club outings.

Local functions are held in the pub throughout the year.

RING OF BELLS
North Bovey, Nr Newton Abbot.   Tel: Moretonhampstead 375

Free House

Map reference number: 51
Situated off the village square of North Bovey, 1½ miles from Moreton-hampstead and 14 miles from Newton Abbot.

Car park. Coaches welcome. Garden at front with benches. Children welcome. Bed & breakfast and full board available in 5 rooms all with hot & cold water.

Worthington E, Double Diamond, Whitbread Tankard, Trophy, Heineken lager and draught Bulmers Strongbow cider available. Good range of snacks and meals served over the bar. Wide selection of food served in the separate restaurant.

A 2-storeyed, long, low stone and cobb thatched building, the *Ring of Bells* probably dates from the 13th century. It was then church property.

The whole pub stands around an attractive, grass forecourt. It has 2 bars, both with low ceilings, original timbers, subdued lighting and period furniture. Carpet throughout makes both bars extremely comfortable. There is a large open fireplace in 1 bar, small paned windows and numerous racing prints on all the walls. The original beams and walls were exposed about 23 years ago having been concealed for centuries.

North Bovey is one of the prettiest and most secluded villages in Devon. It has been voted the tidiest village on many occasions. Both Newton Abbot and Devon & Exeter race-courses are within easy reach.

Okehampton

FOUNTAIN HOTEL
Fore Street, Okehampton.   Tel: Okehampton 2828

Whitbreads

Map reference number: 14
Situated in central Okehampton.

Car park. Bed & breakfast available Easter to October in 10 rooms all with
hot & cold water and teasmaids.

Whitbread best bitter from the wood and keg Tankard available. Home-made
soups, patés, ploughmans, cold meat platters and sandwiches served over
the bar. Dinners served in the separate restaurant.

Built in 1450 of local granite, this inn is now painted. It has 2 bars with
exposed beams, open fireplace and old world décor.

Ottery St Mary

KINGS ARMS HOTEL
Gold Street, Ottery St Mary.   Tel: Ottery St Mary 2879

Devenish

Map reference number: 89
Situated in the centre of Ottery St Mary, just down the road from the
church. 6 miles from Honiton, 6 miles from Sidmouth.

Car park. Coaches by invitation. Small patio. Bed & breakfast and full
board available in 5 double rooms and 2 family rooms all with hot & cold
water. Residents lounge.

Keg Whitbread, Tankard, Devenish Saxon lager, Heineken lager and draught
Guinness available. Complete range of hot and cold snacks served over the
bar. A la carte menu, including steaks, fish, chicken, duckling, gammon,
served in separate restaurant.

Built of stone in 1756 as a coaching inn the *Kings Arms* is situated down the
hill from the church. The old stables to the rear still stand, but are used as
private garages. It is only recently that the archway through which the
coaches drove to the stables has been closed.

The décor in the one large lounge bar is warm and attractive. The bar is named
after the famous event of rolling the tar barrel, performed every year on
5th November. The history and photos of this event surround the walls. There
is a small private bar upstairs.

Paignton

SHIP INN
Manor Road, Paignton.   Tel: Paignton 55842

Free House

Map reference number: 75
Situated in the centre of Preston on the main road to the sea, 1 mile from
Paignton town centre.

Car park.

Wide range of keg and bottled beers available. Sandwiches and basket
meals served over the bar. Steaks, duckling, fish, curries served in the
2 restaurants. One downstairs, the other up.

A large late-Victorian hotel, that has been converted to a Tudor-style interior.
It is painted blue and white outside with twin apexed roof sections and a
lower central section.

The atmosphere is strikingly warm and friendly. 3 bars. Interesting décor.
The busiest pub in Torbay. Discreet background music played.

Pennymoor

CRUWYS ARMS
Pennymoor, Nr Tiverton.   Tel: Cheriton Fitzpaine 347

Free House

Map reference number: 61
Situated 1 mile off the A373 Tiverton to South Molton road. 7 miles to
Tiverton.

Car park.

Keg Double Diamond, Trophy, Tankard and Stella Artois lager available.
Sandwiches, ploughmans, and coffee served over the bar.

Situated 800' above sea-level the *Cruwys Arms* has wonderful views over
Dartmoor. It was built around 1560, with cobb walls and feather-cobbled
forecourt. It is completely unspoilt.

The interior is small, with old beams and open fire in the one bar. There is a
genuine Jacobean screen, a 17th century wooden settle, and lots of highly
polished copper and brass.

Folk singing performed 30 nights of the year.

THE MINERVA
Looe Street, Plymouth.   Tel: Plymouth 69065

Courage

Map reference number: 12
Situated centrally in Plymouth.

Parking in street. Coaches welcome.

Bitter from the wood, keg and draught bitters, Taunton Exhibition cider available. Pasties, pies and rolls served over the bar.

This house was built, mainly with ships' timbers, by a sea captain in 1572. Originally used as a seaman's rest, later becoming a pub, it is thought to be the oldest licensed building in Plymouth. Its name was changed temporarily to *The French Maid* when a documentary on the life story of Agnes Weston, of Sailor's Rest fame, was filmed around the pub.

It has 4 storeys with a slight overhang, and a stained glass first floor window with a picture of Minerva, Greek goddess of wisdom, at centre. The one bar is small but cosy and interesting. The ceiling is low and there is an original fireplace.

The Minerva is conveniently situated for Plymouth Hoe and town centre. Many events and attractions are held in and around Plymouth during the summer season.

WARREN HOUSE INN
Postbridge, Dartmoor.   Tel: Postbridge 88208

Free House

Map reference number: 50
Situated on the B3212 Moretonhampstead to Princetown road. 7 miles from Moretonhampstead, 7 miles from Princetown.

Car park. Coaches welcome. Beer garden, tye-bars for horses. Trekkers welcome. Children's room.

Tankard, Tartan, Worthington E, Double Diamond, Carlsberg lager and Strongbow cider available. Soup, ploughmans, chicken, scampi, fisherman's platter, pies, sandwiches and salads served over the bar. Egon Ronay recommended.

An inn has stood on this site for over 500 years, first on the south side of the road across Dartmoor, now on the north side. It was originally used by miners who worked the tin mines on the moor.

The fire in the inglenook fireplace grate has not gone out for 129 years. The one bar has a low, beamed ceiling, comfortable furnishings and copper ornaments.

JOURNEY'S END INN
Ringmore, Nr Kingsbridge. Tel: Bigbury-on-Sea 205

Free House

Map reference number: 33
Situated down a country lane in Ringmore. It is well-marked but not easy
to find. 8 miles from Kingsbridge, 10 miles from Salcombe.

Car park. Garden. Accommodation available in 5 rooms, all with hot &
cold water.

Wadworth 6X and Old Timer bitters from the wood. Keg Whitbread,
Worthington E, Bass, Red Barrel, Watneys Special, M & B mild and
Mannings of Tuckenhay cider available.

Wide selection of toasted and plain sandwiches, sausages, soups and
scampi served over the bar. Super selection of excellent food served in the
separate restaurant — all fresh and cooked by the landlord's wife. Includes
lobster, quails, steaks, duckling, scampi.

Built originally in 1180 of cobb, the *Journey's End* was first established as
an inn by Elizabeth I. It was here that R. C. Sherriff wrote his play *The
Journey's End*. There are 3 licensed bars all magnificently olde worlde.
Open log fires.

Set in a picture-book village, the inn is within easy reach of numerous
coves and unspoiled beaches. Good sea-fishing, including sharks — river
fishing for trout and salmon, sailing and rough shooting are also available.

Sampford Courtenay

THE NEW INN
Sampford Courtenay, Nr Okehampton. Tel: North Tawton 247

Heavitree

Map reference number: 16
Situated 5 miles out of Okehampton on the A3072 Crediton road.

Car park. Coaches by appointment. Lawn garden with hedges and stream.
Bed & breakfast and full board available in 1 family room, 2 double and 2
single bedrooms.

Draught rough and sweet cider from the wood, keg Tankard, mild, lager,
Worthington E and Trophy available. Mead, apple wine and home-made
gooseberry, elderberry, redcurrant wines and sherry also available.

Complete range of hot & cold snacks, including smoked mackerel,
served over the bar. Full table d'hôte evening meals served in the separate
restaurant.

Established in the 15th century as an inn, the building of thatch and cobb
is much older. The pub is situated in one of Devon's most picturesque
villages — Sampford Courtenay is a past winner of the *Britain in Bloom*
competition and is the 1974 holder of the title *Best Kept Village in
England.*

Sidbury

HARE & HOUNDS INN
Gittisham Common, Sidbury, Nr Sidmouth. Tel: Honiton 2987

Free House

Map reference number: 88
Situated on the edge of the Common at the crossroads of the Honiton and
Sidmouth roads. 3 miles from Honiton and 7 miles from Sidmouth.

Car park. Coaches by appointment. Garden. Children's room.

8 different draught and keg beers, mead available. Snacks available
in all bars.

A long and low white building with a red tiled roof, it was built in the
16th century and extended in the 1930s. Set in a conservation area, the
nearest building is over 3 miles away.

An ideal refuge for highwaymen it was used by bandits in the 18th century
and many strange stories are told about the building. There is a witches'
stone set opposite the pub.

SANDY PARK INN
Sandy Park, Chagford, Dartmoor.   Tel: Chagford 3406

Heavitree

Map reference number: 54
Situated on the A382 Okehampton to Newton Abbot road, 2 miles from Chagford.

Small car park.

Draught Whitbreads best bitter, Tankard, Guinness and Heineken lager available. Recommended by CAMRA. Home-made patés, soups, pies, cold meats and salads, ploughmans, rolls, coffee always available over the bar.

A 15th century thatched cobb and granite building, the *Sandy Park* has been a pub for over 400 years. Previously it was a coaching stop and a blacksmiths was housed in the present-day licensed premises. In fact, the landlord was also always the blacksmith. A tollgate was situated just around the corner from the pub.

Altered in 1938 the one bar still retains its genuine décor and atmosphere. It has an open fire, oak trestles, a dartboard and a set of table skittles.

A cosy, country pub that is highly recommended.

BLUE BALL INN

Sidford, Nr Sidmouth. Tel: Sidmouth 4062

Devenish

Map reference number: 87
Situated on the B3052 Exeter to Lyme Regis road, at the eastern end of
Sidford village.

Car park. Coaches by invitation. Children's room. Large garden. Barbecue
area.

Draught Devenish bitter, Wessex IPA, Guinness, keg Tankard, Saxon, Viking
and Heineken lagers. Large range of hot and cold snacks served over the
bar.

1585 is the date of construction of this thatched, stone and cobb building.
Salcombe Regis was the last Cavalier stronghold in the area and the pub is
believed to have strong connections with the Civil War. The pub was
originally owned by the Balle family, who probably gave it its name. More
probably it was named after a blue pint, or a measure less than a pint,
which was made illegal in 1890.

There are 2 bars, beamed with enormous old open fireplaces. The large
lounge has recently been converted from a cowshed.

South Brent

WOODPECKER
South Brent, Nr Totnes.   Tel: South Brent 2125

Free House

Map reference number: 29
Situated in South Brent to the west of the A38, 8 miles from Totnes and
13 miles from Torbay.

Car park. Lawn garden. Accommodation to be offered after alterations
completed.

All popular beers available — Wadworth bitter from the wood to be
installed soon. Fine selection of home-made snacks served over the bar.
Cosy and popular restaurant with good food at reasonable prices.

The *Woodpecker* is a picturesque English pub that sits very prettily beside
the new A38. Parts date back from 1750.

The interior is imposing, cosy and popular — the décor has to be seen to be
believed. There is an open log fire, exposed beams and an old porch.

South Molton

GEORGE HOTEL
Broad Street, South Molton. Tel: South Molton 2514

Free House

Map reference number: 21
Situated in the centre of South Molton which is on the main A361
Taunton to Barnstaple road.

Car park. Coaches by invitation. Garden. Bed & breakfast and full
board available in 11 rooms, 1 with private bath, all with hot & cold
water. Children welcome. Residents' lounge.

Whitbread Tankard, Trophy, Worthington E, Watneys special, Ind Coope
best bitter, Carling Black Label, Stella Artois lager and Hancocks cider —
brewed and bottled 3 miles away — available. Full cold meat buffet, table
d'hôte menu (lunchtimes) and plated steaks (evenings) served over the bar.
Table d'hôte and à la carte menus, including flambé dishes, served in the
separate restaurant.

Dating back from the 13th century, the *George* was originally a coaching
inn. Every Thursday, Market Day, farmers of the Exmoor area come to the
hotel to bargain and deal in the bars. The hotel is noted for its friendly staff
and customers. Undergoing a face lift at present.

OXENHAM ARMS
South Zeal, Nr Okehampton.   Tel: Sticklepath 244

Free House

Map reference number: 26
Situated 4 miles from Okehampton just off the A30 Exeter road.

Car park. Large lawn garden. Bed & breakfast and full board available in
9 rooms, 5 with private bathrooms.

Whitbread Tankard, Courage IPA, Stella Artois lager and full range of
bottled beers available. Extensive range of hot and cold snacks served over
the bar. Table d'hôte and à la carte luncheons and dinners served in the
separate restaurant. Egon Ronay and Ashley Courtenay recommended.

First licensed in 1477 the *Oxenham Arms* is a unique inn with many historic associations. It lies in a valley on an old coaching route and is believed
to have been built by lay monks in the 12th century. Sometime after the
dissolution of the Monasteries it became the Dower House of the
Burgoyne family whose heiress carried it to the Oxenham family, after
whom the inn is named. Scheduled as an Ancient Monument.

The one bar has the décor and atmosphere of a first-class ancient English
coaching inn. It has flagstone floors, exposed Dartmoor granite walls,
beams and an open log fire. The rest of the house is as historic and interesting as the bar.

Nestling at the base of the celebrated Cawsand Beacon, the *Oxenham
Arms* is ideally sited for exploring Dartmoor. Fishing, golfing, riding facilities are all within easy reach.

Spreyton

TOM COBLEY TAVERN
Spreyton, Nr Crediton.   Tel: Whiddon Down 314

Free House

Map reference number: 25
Situated in the centre of Spreyton, equidistant from Okehampton
and Crediton.

Car park. Coaches by arrangement. Lawn garden. Skittle alley. Bed
& breakfast available in 4 rooms, all with hot & cold water.

Double Diamond, Tavern, Whitbread Trophy, Tankard, Heineken lager and
cider available. Snacks and hot dishes — scampi, steaks, curries — served over
the bar. Evening meals by arrangement.

Built in the 16th century, this inn was originally called the *White Hart.*
Thomas Cobley — of Uncle Tom Cobley fame — was born in the parish in
1762 and around the year 1800 the famous journeys to Widecombe Fair
started, the travellers probably assembling at the inn. Tom Cobley died in
1844 and his grave can still be seen in Spreyton churchyard.

To commemorate Cobley and the journeys, the pub was re-named, a
plaque relating the tale was hung outside and the interior decorated with
momentoes of the occasion. There is a thatched bar and an open fire in
the Tom Cobley bar. The Lounge Bar is larger, newer and mainly used for
private parties.

Spreyton is the highest village in Devon apart from those on Dartmoor, and
previously the church tower was painted white to help guide passing ships
in the Bristol Channel. Trees and buildings now block the view.

THE SEA TROUT INN

Staverton, Nr Totnes. Tel: Staverton 274

Free House

Map reference number: 44
Situated in Staverton, 4 miles north-west of Totnes.

Car park. Patio with seats and fish pond. Bed & breakfast available in 5 double rooms and 4 single rooms. 4 rooms situated in annexe.

Keg Worthington E, Double Diamond, Whitbread Tankard, Guinness, M & B mild, Heineken, Stella Artois lager and locally made cider from the wood. Home-made steak & kidney pie, gammon, seafood, salads, soups, hot meals with chips and sandwiches served over the bar. Salad bar and table d'hôte menu served in separate restaurant lunchtimes. English and Continental menu served in the evenings. Highly recommended.

A cottage-style building of white stone with black frames and slate roof, *The Sea Trout* is set in a picturesque village. It dates back to the 15th century when it was owned by the Church and used as a rest house by monks during the building of Buckfast Abbey. Previously called the *Church House Inn* its name was changed 18 years ago to commemorate the fine sea trout available in the nearby River Dart.

Although it has been developed the pub still retains a country inn atmosphere and décor. The lounge bar is informal and relaxed, with comfortable furnishings and open log fires. The small public bar is frequented by local cider drinkers and dart players. The restaurant is wood panelled.

Fishing, walking, riding, sailing and golf can all be organised from *The Sea Trout*.

Starcross

THE GALLEON INN
Starcross, Nr Exeter.   Tel: Starcross 412

Whitbreads

Map reference number:79
Situated on the main Exeter to Dawlish road, 7 miles from Exeter.

Car park. Coaches welcome. Children's room.

Draught and keg Whitbread beers , Stella Artois and Heineken lagers served over the bar. Soup, sandwiches, chicken, scampi, cod, scallops and salads served over the bar. Steaks, lobster, trout, duck, chicken, gammon served in the separate restaurant.

Dating from 1490 and then known as the *Ship* this inn was the haunt of local fishermen. It is built of cobb with leaded windows. Large open fireplace, showing hand cleft oak beam, exposed timbers and rough stonework are the main features of the interior.

Starcross is a well-known yachting and fishing centre and the sight of Brunel's atmospheric railway pumping station.

Sticklepath

THE RISING SUN
Sticklepath, Nr Okehampton.   Tel: Sticklepath 215

Free House

Map reference number:15
Situated 4 miles east of Okehampton on the main A30 Exeter road.

Car park. Coaches by arrangement. Patio. Children's room.

Draught Whitbread best bitter, keg Double Diamond, Tankard, special bitter, special mild, Guinness, Heineken lager and farmhouse cider available. Steaks, plaice, chicken, home-made pies, soups, paté, pasties, ploughmans and sandwiches served over the bar.

The Rising Sun was originally a miner's pub with patrons who worked the nearby, now disused, copper mine. Partly 200-300 years old and partly modern, the pub has marvellous views to Exmoor at the front and to Dartmoor at the rear. It backs onto a common.

The main bar has a long, fine oak counter and has a beamed, old world atmosphere. The lounge is cosy and modern.

JACK RUSSEL
Swimbridge, Nr Barnstaple.   Tel: Swimbridge 306

Watney Mann

Map reference number: 18
Situated on the main A361 Barnstaple to Taunton road, 4½ miles from
Barnstaple and 9 miles from South Molton.

Car park. Bed & breakfast available in 4 rooms, all with hot & cold water.

Keg Watney beers and lager available. Sandwiches and basket meals served
over the bar. Steaks, chops, fish, varied hors d'oeuvres and desserts served
in the restaurant.

A long, low building painted white, it has shuttered windows, hanging
flower baskets and flower beds. It is the only pub in the centre of the
village.

For 48 years Swimbridge had the legendary Reverend Jack Russel as its
vicar. The inn is thus named after him and a photograph, over 100 years
old, hangs in the Lounge Bar.

There are 2 bars, both in good decorative order after renovation during
the later part of 1974. There are open fires and exposed beams.

KINGS ARMS INN

Tedburn St Mary, Nr Exeter.   Tel: Tedburn St Mary 224

Free House

Map reference number: 58
Situated 7 miles west of Exeter on the main A30 road to Okehampton.

Car park. Bed & breakfast available in 3 treble and 3 double rooms, all
with hot & cold water.

Whitbreads best bitter from the wood, Watneys Red Barrel, Whitbreads
Tankard, special mild, Heineken lager and Devon cider made in the village
available. Full range of snacks served over the bar. Table d'hôte luncheons
and à la carte dinners served in the separate restaurant. Egon Ronay
recommended.

Built in 1630 and originally a coaching house the *Kings Arms* is constructed
of cobb and oak beams. A 1639 Charles I coin was found in the garden and
is displayed.

There is one bar with low ceiling, stone floor, old beams, large open fireplace
and collection of horse brasses. It has a genuine, friendly old world atmosphere. The restaurant is cosy and intimate.

The village of Tedburn St Mary was originally known as Taphouse after
the beer on tap at this pub, and it is shown as Taphouse on various old maps.
It is a good centre for touring both north and south Devon. It is also an
ideal overnight stop for travellers on their way to Cornwall.

Stockland

KINGS ARMS INN
Stockland, Nr Honiton.   Tel: Stockland 361

Bass Charrington

Map reference number: 93
Situated in Stockland village, 6 miles from Honiton and 6 miles from
Axminster.

Car park. Coaches by invitation. Lawn garden with flower borders. Bed &
breakfast and full board available in 3 rooms, all with hot & cold water.

Keg Worthington E, Brew XI, Bass special, Toby bitter and Carling lager
available. Full range of hot and cold snacks and meals served over the bar.
Dinners served in the separate restaurant by arrangement.

Built in the 1600s in a super rural situation, the *Kings Arms* is a thatched
cobb house. There are 3 bars, including one in the Skittle Alley, all with
exposed beams and inglenook fireplaces. The Skittle Alley is reputed to be
the oldest in East Devon.

Tiverton

WHITE BALL INN
Bridge Street, Tiverton.   Tel: Tiverton 2256

Whitbreads

Map reference number: 62
Situated on the west bank of the River Exe on the main exit route from
Tiverton to the west.

Car park. Lawn garden. Children admitted to coffee room. Bed & breakfast
available in 5 rooms, all with hot & cold water.

Draught Trophy, keg Tankard, Heineken and Stella Artois lagers available.
Recommended by CAMRA. Sandwiches, pasties, ploughmans served over
the bar. Good small à la carte menu, prepared from local produce, served
in the separate restaurant.

Rebuilt around 1795 after a fire, the *White Ball* still retains late Georgian
windows in a stucco facade and a cobbled yard. A scheduled building.

The lounge bar has been restored to a Georgian coaching inn atmosphere
with open fire, some beams and a large interesting collection of willow
pattern china and old prints. The public bar is of late Victorian style. The
pub is used by some old Devonian characters whose accent and phrasiology
are of interest to visitors.

Torbryan

OLD CHURCH HOUSE INN
Torbryan, Ipplepen, Nr Newton Abbot.   Tel: Ipplepen 812372

Free House

Map reference number: 45
Situated off the Newton Abbot to Totnes road, through Ipplepen village
into Torbryan. 5 miles from Newton Abbot.

Car park. Coaches by invitation. Garden.

Keg Whitbread Tankard, Watneys Starlight, Double Diamond, Worthington
E, Tartan, Ansells mild, Carlsberg lager, mead and rough cider available.
Large assortment of snacks and light meals served over the bar. Full à la
carte menu served in the separate restaurant.

The very famous *Old Church House Inn* was built in 1400, of stone and
cobb, on the site of a very ancient cottage, the remains of which can still
be seen. At that time it was church property and was used to house workmen engaged on the restoration of the church next door, which dates from
the 8th or 9th century. Beer was brewed on the premises and there was also
a bakehouse. The old oven can still be seen. It was also the meeting place of
famous owners of cock-fighters and it is recorded that in 1450 a fight took
place with £1900 for a stake. Many Royal personages stayed at the inn
including Henry VIII.

The atmosphere in the 3 bars has remained almost unchanged over the
centuries. Items of interest to note are the magnificent oak panelling, the
original stone of the sun-dial set in the floor, a set of skittles over 400
years old, ancient cider kegs, inglenook fireplace and fine Saxon doorway.
The inn is also reputed to have its own ghost.

HOLE IN THE WALL
6 Park Lane, Strand, Torquay.   Tel: Torquay 22292

Courage

Map reference number: 73
Situated in central Torquay off up the hill from one of the main streets.

Parking in town. Coaches welcome. Bed & breakfast available. Range of snacks served over the bar.

Over 400 years old, the *Hole in the Wall* is reputed to be the oldest pub in Torquay. It is believed to have had strong connections with smugglers in the past, who used underground passages from the beach to the pub to move their contraband from the boats.

The 2 bars are period with a large collection of knickknacks on display. There are exposed beams, a log fire and a pebbled floor.

Situated close to Torquay harbour.

Topsham

BRIDGE INN
Topsham, Exeter.   Tel: Topsham 3862

Free House

Map reference number: 80
Situated on the main Exeter to Exmouth road, by the River Clyst and 5
miles from Exeter.

Car park. Coaches by invitation.

Wadworth Old Timer and 6X bitters from the wood, draught Worthington E and
IPA, keg Tankard and Heineken lager and mead available. Ploughmans lunches
with rye or wholemeal bread served over the bar.

Originally a lodging house for the masons who built the Cathedral at Exeter,
it later became a brewery and a coaching house. Constructed of cobb and
stone, now pink-washed, it also had close associations with smuggling and
illicit trading, because of its ideal river position.

The small bar has a low ceiling and period furniture. Private parties held in
the old malt house adjacent.

Totnes

ROYAL SEVEN STARS HOTEL
Totnes.   Tel: Totnes 862125

Free House

Map reference number: 41
Situated in the centre of Totnes.

Car park. Coaches by appointment. Bed & breakfast available in 18 rooms,
8 with private bath.

Draught Bass, keg Whitbread Tankard, Double Diamond, Guinness and Skol
lager available. Basket meals served over the bar. Table d'hôte and à la carte
menus served in separate but adjoining restaurant. Grill bar and buttery
open in summer.

An attractrive old coaching inn dating from 1660, the *Royal Seven Stars* is
set in the middle of Totnes overlooking the River Dart. It has a large Tudor
porch.

There is one principal bar with beams and log fire. There is also a ballroom
suite large enough to cater for 140 persons. Dinner/dances and cabaret shows
are held every Saturday during summer season. Olde Tyme Music Hall also
held occasionally.

THE OLD SMITHY INN

Welcombe, Nr Bideford.   Tel: Morewenstow 305

Free House

Map reference number: 1
Situated west of the A39, above the surf beach of Welcombe Mouth, 18 miles from Bideford and 12 miles from Bude.

Car park. Coaches welcome. Lawn garden. Bed & breakfast and full board available in 1 double room and 1 single room.

Keg Watney, Worthington, Double Diamond, Tankard, Tartan bitters, Carlsberg lager, mead and draught cider available. Basket meals, toasted sandwiches, salads, steaks, home-made pies, ploughmans served over the bar.

Set in a designated area of outstanding natural beauty on cliffs above the Atlantic, *The Old Smithy Inn* is a thatched, 13th century stone and cobb building. It was once the home of the local smithy, a man named Kaleb, who is depicted on the inn sign with his anvil and hammer. Kaleb was an expert at pulling teeth as well as shoeing horses. The building was first licensed in 1962.

This is a typical Devon country inn, tastefully furnished and with open log fires and beams. An original bread oven remains alongside one of the fireplaces. The ghost of a Cavalier, wounded at the Battle of Stamford Hill, and who died in the inn, is said to haunt the bars.

Organ music played on Saturday nights.

Upottery

SIDMOUTH ARMS
Upottery, Nr Honiton.   Tel: Upottery 252

Whitbreads

Map reference number: 92
Situated in Upottery village, 5½ miles from Honiton and 15 miles
from the coast.

Car park. Coaches by invitation. Lawn garden with trees and flowers,
overlooking the valley. Skittle alley. Bed & breakfast and full board
available in 5 double and 1 single room, all with hot & cold water.

Draught bitter from old-fashioned pumps, keg bitter, mild and various local
concoctions available. Hot pies, basket meals and salads served over the
bar. Full à la carte menu, and special Sunday roast lunches, served in the
separate restaurant.

Built in 1600 of local stone, the *Sidmouth Arms* is set in the centre of a
delightful village. It is named after the local Sidmouth family, and particular-
ly after the first Lord Sidmouth who was given his title for reportedly
curing Charles III of his mental illness.

There are 3 bars. The bar in the Skittle Alley has old beams and displays
heads of the Lords' Sidmouth. The lounge has an old world atmosphere
with an open log fire and beams. Skittle weeks are often held and all are
invited to play.

Widecombe-in-the-Moor

THE OLD INN
Widecombe-in-the-Moor, Newton Abbot. Tel: Widecombe 207

Free House

Map reference number: 49
Situated in Dartmoor National Park.

Car park. Coaches welcome. Garden. Children's room. Bed & breakfast
available in 3 rooms. Evening meals to order.

Draught and keg beers, cider from the wood, mead, vintage cider available.
Basket meals, ploughmans, pasties, toasted and plain sandwiches served
over the bar. Meals to order served in the separate restaurant.

A 14th century pub situated in a delightful old Dartmoor village. *The Old
Inn* has 4 bars, all timbered with open log fires, exposed beams and stone
walls. The ghosts of Uncle Tom Cobley and All are said to haunt the
building.

Wilmington

WHITE HART
Wilmington, Nr Honiton.   Tel: Wilmington 226

Bass Charrington

Map reference number: 94
Situated on the A35, 3 miles east of Honiton.

Car park.

Worthington E, Bass special and Carling Black Label lager available. Pies, pasties, rolls, sandwiches, ploughmans served over the bar.

All that you might expect a Devon inn to be — 16th century, thatched, cobb walls, interesting shape, bar high inglenook fireplace, exposed beams and low ceilings.

The bars are friendly and cosy and have an interesting display of horse brasses, prints and antiques. The old skittle alley retains its original clay base.

Withycombe Raleigh

THE HOLLY TREE INN
Withycombe Raleigh, Exmouth.   Tel: Exmouth 73440

Devenish

Map reference number: 83
Situated just off the main Exeter to Exmouth road in the village of Withycombe.

Car park. Coaches welcome. Beer garden. Bed & breakfast with evening meal available in 6 double and 2 single rooms.

Worthington E from the wood, Devenish IPA from the wood, keg Saxon bitter, Whitbread Tankard, draught Viking and Heineken lagers and Devon rough cider from the wood. Hot foods — scampi, chicken, plaice, steaks — sandwiches, salads, pies, ploughmans served over the bar.

Attractive appearance with rough-cast walls and green paintwork. Being the most popular pub in the Exmouth area you'd expect the atmosphere to be good — and it is. Nicely decorated.

¾ mile from the beach. 2 minutes walk from pitch & putt course, bowling green and tennis court.

Woodbury

THE WHITE HART INN

Woodbury, Nr Exeter.   Tel: Woodbury 32221

Bass Charrington

Map reference number: 82
Situated almost equidistant between Exeter and Exmouth, 5 miles
from Exeter.

Car park. Coaches welcome. Lawn garden.

Draught Worthington E, keg Bass and Toby bitter available. Hot and cold
snacks, pasties and coffee served over the bar.

Built at the turn of the 15th century *The White Hart* was built within a
few yards of the gates to the Saxon Parish church of St. Swithun. Residents
of Woodbury and patrons of this inn have played their parts in history —
the Battle of Agincourt, local baronial struggles, the Civil War, the 2 world
wars. Many stories of heroism and tragedy must have been swopped in this
inn's bars.

There are 2 bars, both cosy with log fires. Good company and atmosphere.
Situated close to the ancient castle of Woodbury.

Index

SAILING BOATS OF THE WORLD.

a guide to classes

The *first* complete guide to all kinds of sailing boats from all over the world.

Over 1100 dinghies, sailing surfboards, racers, cruisers, motor-cruisers – both multihulls and monohulls – are described in detail, giving full specifications, outline drawing, suppliers, fittings and price. 900 more are listed in brief.

This is a book
- for yachtsmen, whether owners or dreamers, to simply browse through

- for yacht clubs for members to consult and settle arguments

- for libraries where its comprehensive list of boats and manufacturers' will be constantly referred to

- for potential buyers who will find this a mine of information on designs currently available

1252 pages.   full colour section
ISBN 0 220 66650 4

only £5.50

Bayard Books c/o Business Books Ltd, Mercury House, Waterloo Road, London SE 1

BAYARD BOOKS

c/o Business Books Limited
Mercury House Waterloo Road
London SE1 8UL 01-928 3388

Bayard Books is publishing, sponsored by Alka-Seltzer, a series of paperback guides to the pleasantest pubs of most of the counties in the United Kingdom.

Each guide contains information on drinks, food, accommodation available, setting, history and local attractions. A map of the county pinpoints the position of each pub. There is an introduction to each county by a local expert, an alphabetical list of every pub featured and a list of each village or town mentioned.

All are illustrated by Myerscough.

Already available

PUBS OF DEVON
0 220 66655 5   96pp   60p

PUBS OF KENT
0 220 66652 0   96pp   60p

PUBS OF SUSSEX
0 220 66651 2   96pp   60p

Coming soon

**PUBS OF HAMPSHIRE & THE ISLE
OF WIGHT**
0 220 66656 3   128pp   75p